The

Addicks

cartoons

By Richard Redden

NEWS BROKER SERVICES

First published in 2003 by News Broker Services,
48 Station Road, West Wickham, Kent BR4 0PR

ISBN 0-9544745-0-3

A catalogue record for this book is also
available from the British Library

Printed and bound in Great Britain by
Martins the Printers Limited, Sea View Works, Spittal,
Berwick upon Tweed TD15 1RS

Author's dedication:

This book is dedicated to the memory of my friend Chris Thomas.
As boys in the 1950s, we used to cycle together from Bromley, Kent,
to The Valley on Saturday matchdays. Chris died, after a long illness,
on the morning of the day Charlton celebrated their First Division
Championship and their return to the FA Premiership, in the game
against Ipswich Town at The Valley – Saturday, April 29, 2000.
I also dedicate this book to my young grandchildren, Max and Bonnie,
in the fond hope that they too, like my three children, William, James
and Katherine, will grow up to become Addicks.

THE FOUNDING YEARS OF CHARLTON ATHLETIC

SEASON 1905/6
Friendlies
GROUND: SIEMENS MEADOW

SEASON 1906/7
Lewisham League Division 3 Winners
GROUND: SIEMENS MEADOW

SEASON 1907/8
Lewisham League Division 2 Winners
(Winners Division 2B, overall winners Division 2)
Woolwich League Division 2 Winners
Woolwich Cup, lose in 1st Round
GROUND: WOOLWICH COMMON

SEASON 1908/9
Lewisham League Division 1 Winners
Blackheath League Division 2 Winners
Woolwich Cup Winners
Reserve team compete in Woolwich League
Division 3A
GROUND: POUND PARK

SEASON 1909/10
Woolwich League Division 1 Winners
Blackheath League Division 1 Winners
(There was a senior division to this league)
Woolwich Cup Winners
Charlton Charity Cup Finalists
GROUND: POUND PARK

SEASON 1910/11
Woolwich League Division 1 Winners
Blackheath League Division 1 Winners
Woolwich Cup Winners
London Junior Cup, reach 4th Round
GROUND: POUND PARK

SEASON 1911/12
Southern Suburban League,
First Division (Eastern Section) Winners
Southern Suburban League
First Division Winners overall
(There was a senior division to this league)
Woolwich League Division 1 Runners-up
Charlton Charity Cup Winners
London Junior Cup, reach 3rd Round
GROUND: POUND PARK

SEASON 1912/13
Southern Suburban League,
First Division (Eastern Section) Winners
Southern Suburban League
First Division Winners overall
Woolwich League Division 1 Winners
Woolwich Cup Winners
Charlton Charity Cup Finalists
London Junior Cup, reach 5th Round
GROUND: POUND PARK

SEASON 1913/14
Southern Suburban League, Senior
Division (Eastern Section) Winners
Southern Suburban League, Senior
Division Runners-up overall
London League Division 1 Runners-up
(There were two senior divisions to this league)
London Senior Cup, reach 4th Round
Kent Senior Cup, reach 1st Round Proper
Reserve team disqualified in 2nd Round of
Charlton Charity Cup and in 2nd Round, Kent Junior
Cup. Reach 2nd Round, London Junior Cup
GROUND: ANGERSTEIN LANE

SEASON 1914/15
Friday, March 19, 1915, announced that club
was suspending operations because of wartime
Club competed this season in:
London League Premier Division
(Amateur Section)
London Senior Cup, reach 5th Qualifying
Round (but game awarded to
Walthamstow Grange after Charlton failed
to turn up)
Southern Suburban League, Senior Division (Eastern
Section) - entered but competition called off at start
of season because of war
Reserve team competed in London League Division 1.
Also reached 2nd Round of London Intermediate Cup
Club entered FA Cup for first time losing
to Dartford in First Qualifying Round
Replay
Club entered FA Amateur Cup for first
time losing to Grays Athletic in First
Round Proper
GROUND: ANGERSTEIN LANE

AUTHOR'S ACKNOWLEDGEMENTS

As with my previous Charlton history, Valley of Tears, Valley of Joy, I would warmly like to thank the staff of the Greenwich Local History Library whom I have got to know well over the years. Their courtesy, kindliness and cheerfulness were unfailing and exceptional. Greenwich Borough has a tremendous asset not only in the archive material stored but the people who manage and care for it, so this time I would like to acknowledge them personally - Julian Watson, Frances Ward, Jenny O'Keefe, and Caroline Warhurst who has since left the staff. I would also like to thank Parrett & Neves Limited of Whitstable, who still hold the title to the defunct Kentish Independent. Although copyright to the cartoons has long expired, I contacted the company when I set out on this project, and got their blessing and approval. By reviving the cartoons, I also hope I am reviving memories of the old Independent. I am indebted to Colin Cameron for kindly giving up his time to check the historical accuracy of the book's contents. Colin is the Charlton guru on all historical facts and statistics and has published two marvellous reference books on Charlton history – Home & Away with Charlton Athletic 1920-1992 and the Valiant 500. Robin Rickwood also deserves my special thanks. Robin grew up in the 1920s and 1930s in the cradle of Charlton Athletic, the streets by the modern day Thames Barrier, and twice took me round to point out and describe the sites of the old landmarks of the club, such as Arthur Bryan's fishmongers at 77 East Street (now Eastmoor Street), the Crown and Prince of Wales pubs, and the Blundell Mission opposite the fishmongers. My lifelong friend and lifelong Charlton supporter Gordon Ducker, with Robin's help, took photographs of the sites. I am also grateful to him and to my son James for proofreading the book. My thanks also go to Edward Hampton, son of the pre First World War goalkeeper Albert Hampton, Steve Bridge who pointed me to further information about the founding of the Addicks in 1905, Mike Cassar of Express Newspapers who gave me valuable technical advice on the scanning of the cartoons, John Lawrence of Dulwich Hamlet for information about the Southern Suburban League, John Coulter of Lewisham Library Local Studies for information about the Catford Southend club, and to my wife Susan for her very practical support and encouragement, especially when our two-year-old granddaughter Bonnie delayed the book by singlehandedly demolishing the operating system of my Mac computer. Last and not least, I also have to say a very special thank you to Andrew Mercer, the grandson of the Addicker, Arthur Bryan, and his family, all devoted Charlton fans. Andrew is keenly aware of the club's early history through his family connections and has helped and encouraged me throughout. This book is very much a tribute to his grandfather who bequeathed to Charlton the club's so very distinctive nickname – the Addicks.

TECHNICAL NOTE

The 56 cartoons in this book are enhanced in size from single column originals in the Kentish Independent from 1908 to 1915. I had intended to use high quality photographic copies of all cartoons for scanning into the book. However, during the course of writing, some volumes of the Kentish Independent at the British Library Newspaper Library were withdrawn because of wear and damage (these years also cover Arsenal's time as Woolwich Arsenal). Consequently, I had to use microfilm from the library and also from Greenwich Local History Library. There were two problems in this – firstly dust and scratching of the microfilm, and secondly the fact that some of the microfilm was shot to a dark exposure which eliminated some of the detail of the cartoons. I have tried to use Adobe Photoshop to tidy up the affected cartoons as far as possible but inevitably the standard of reproduction varies between the photographic copies and the microfilm copies. The width of penstroke of the cartoonist understandably also varied over the seven years, with some of the cartoons having a heavier, much blacker look. The captions are the original ones.

O n Millennium Eve, I knew there was only place I wanted to go to celebrate the coming of the new century and the new Millennium. With my wife I made my way down the streets to the Thames Barrier and the great river itself to celebrate. Those streets and the area by the Barrier were where the Charlton Athletic club was born. And for better or for worse, I had spent most of my lifetime supporting the club. That support had mostly been in times of failure and decline culminating in the nightmares of 1984 when the club was just 35 minutes away from extinction and of 1985 when the club lost its Valley home.

My wife Susan is not a football fan but she gamely came with me, and together with about 20 other hardy souls we watched the lights shimmer around the Millennium Dome down river as the Millennium came in.

In the distance, we could see the fireworks exploding all along the Thames in central London. And across the river, in West Ham territory, another mighty firework display erupted.

I communed with the spirits of those youngsters, living in a grim, disease-ridden and desperately poor area of Thameside, who founded the club 95 years before. And I wondered what they would have made of it all – of how their stretch of the river had changed beyond all recognition, of the shining new Valley just a mile away, and of the club's rise once again to the top level of English football.

When I wrote Charlton's first-ever full history, Valley of Tears, Valley of Joy, I first came across the cartoons in the Kentish Independent in the pre-First World War period. I always resolved to return to that era and look at it in more detail. Alas statistics, especially league tables and results, are so patchy that it is impossible to do a conventional history but I hope that the narrative form I have followed, based on the cartoons, will give readers a flavour and an understanding of the club's early days – and in particular of how Charlton Athletic came to be called the Addicks.

Richard Redden

The Addick legend - as it grew in pictures

Forever etched on the history of Charlton Athletic Football Club will be the seven years of exile from The Valley – first at Selhurst Park and then at Upton Park. But during those times of desolation and unhappiness, a strange thing happened. Somehow, no-one quite knows how, the club revived its unique and historic nickname: the Addicks.

It was a nickname that dated almost from the time of the club's founding in 1905. But in truth, before the Selhurst days, the name had long since really died. Throughout the postwar period, it had barely been heard.

In the 1930s, partly through the misguidedness of the club's own supporters' club, the artificial name of the Robins was invented for the club – although it was the nickname of several other clubs.

But then the Red Red Robin song was glorified by the famous 1940/50s band leader, Billy Cotton, and so the new name stuck.

The lack of uniqueness of the Robin name led to its own decline until, in a highly dubious fan competition in the mid 1960s, the awful name of the Valiants was chosen – a feeble pun on The Valley. But another club also shared that one – Port Vale.

It was the trauma of the move away from The Valley in 1985 and the fans' heroic and ultimately successful attempt to return to The Valley that led them to look back deep into their own history.

And that history was of teenage boys playing football by the Thames in working class streets in what is now an industrial area by the Thames Barrier. They played their football field on a piece of wasteland by the Thames called Siemens Meadow or the Brickfields. And from that playing on waste ground, the 15-year-old boys formed Charlton Athletic.

Their success was almost immediate and they soon acquired a distinctive nickname based on their South London accents – Addicks from the Haddock fish.

Since no seawater haddock fish could ever possibly have found its way to the Thames, which flowed just yards away from the boys' first pitch, why did this name arise?

It was because of what we would term today one of the club's first 'sponsors', the local fishmonger who took an interest in the boys. He was Arthur Bryan, who ran a shop in one of the streets where the boys lived – East Street.

Arthur treated the team and visitors to fish and chip meals – and he took to brandishing a haddock on a pole at Charlton Athletic matches.

He is the fishmonger – the Addicker – on whom the cartoons in this book are based. They appeared in the Kentish Independent between the years 1908 to 1915.

The Kentish Independent is now defunct but it was then the leading paper in the area and gave Charlton Athletic much wider coverage than its rivals – all, too, now disappeared. Who the cartoonist was I do not know, despite much effort to discover his identity. That is a mystery in the sands of time. Perhaps this book will help identify him.

Jolly although the cartoons are, there is also a sadness. For the Great War was looming and they actually ended in the war itself – alongside, on the same page of the Kentish Independent, of pictures of the first casualties of the Woolwich and Greenwich area in that terrible war.

Whoever the cartoonist was, he left us a unique record of the Charlton club and for that we must warmly thank him down the course of almost a century. Arthur Bryan's descendants we do know however, and the grandson of the original Addicker, Andrew Mercer, is one of the club's most fervent supporters.

At the end of this book we describe the history of the Bryans and their neighbours the Buddens, and the contributions of many others in that riverside community to the founding of the Addicks.

Drawing the teeth of the military's medical men

Although team photographs date from 1905/6, the very first season of Charlton's existence, none appears to have been published in these years before the First World War. There were the occasional football action photographs in the Independent of those days – but they were of Woolwich Arsenal at their Manor Ground in Plumstead before their infamous move away from Woolwich to North London in 1913.

The first public, but non-photographic, depiction of Charlton Athletic came in these cartoons. The first one appeared in the Kentish Independent of Friday, November 6, 1908, relating to the Charlton game of the previous Saturday, October 31.

The Charlton Athletic team actually competed in two leagues, which was not unusual for teams at the time. The leagues were the Lewisham League, which the boys had entered in 1906 – their first league – and the Blackheath League. In this 1908/9 season, they played in Division I of the Lewisham League and Division II of the Blackheath League (really the third division since there was a Senior Division above Division I).

The Charlton area was close by the big military bases of Woolwich, and many of Charlton Athletic's first opponents were military teams – in league, cup and friendlies.

This cartoon alludes to a game at home in the Blackheath League against the Royal Army Medical Corps which Charlton won by 8-0 with a hat-trick from Harry 'Razor' Calcutt, goals from Arthur Ellis, Fred 'Snowy' Marshall and A. Townsend (alas, Christian names were not given in the Independent) and two the visiting centre half put through his own goal – a painful extraction indeed for the R.A.M.C. Home for Charlton this season was Pound Park, close by the chalkpit site of the future Valley.

Extractions from the R.A.M.C. by the Haddocks (Charlton Athletic)

October 31, 1908

First appearance of the Addick creates a stink

In this cartoon, the Addicker, the Charlton fishmonger, makes his first appearance as the symbol of the club. Obviously news of Arthur Bryan's fervent backing of Charlton Athletic had reached the offices of the Kentish Independent and its cartoonist – as perhaps had the smell of the Addicks.

Besides the many army teams in the area, most of the local churches had their own teams, and in this game Charlton found themselves up against Plumstead St. Paul's of the South London Church League in an away tie in the second round of the Woolwich Cup.

There had been a big split in church football in South London in 1906 with the Free Church teams breaking away from the South London Church League to form their own Woolwich and District Free Church League. This was hardly surprising since the league constitution had provided for a permanent majority of Church of England clubs.

Charlton scored three goals in quick succession in the second half to win 3-0, Eddie Marshall (younger brother of Fred), A. Townsend and Arthur Ellis the scorers. In keeping with playing a church team, Charlton found the game a very clean one with just two fouls in the entire match.

It was a church weekend for the Addicks as their reserves were away to St. Mary's Rectory in Division IIIA of the Woolwich League. This was the first season before the Great War that Charlton ran a reserve team but it lasted just a season. Not until 1913-14 was another reserve side formed.

The second game against a church side was not quite so peaceful. With the Charlton reserves losing two-nil, the referee stopped the game five minutes from time "for no apparent cause and this caused much dissatisfaction", according to the Kentish Independent report.

St. Paul of Plumstead was completely "overcome" by the "Haddocks"

November 28, 1908

Fishmonger loses addick in pantomime of a match

The Kentish Independent cartoonist did not just confine himself to the first teams of the area's junior clubs. He illustrated reserve games as well. The fishmonger made his second appearance in the paper's pages when Charlton reserves played a friendly at home at Pound Park to Woolwich Albion.

According to Charlton's report in the paper, "the reserves had a proper pantomime team out, and it was surprising to find that the Albion could not win by more than a very doubtful penalty goal". Here the striped shirted Woolwich Albion player plays the pantomime villain on the fishmonger.

Meanwhile, in Division I of the Lewisham League, the first team endured a non event. They were away to Braby's Ironworks "but after dressing and arriving on the so-called playing pitch, it was found to be nothing better than a rubbish shoot, and as soon as the referee saw it, he decided that it was simply impossible to play thereon".

The first team were also without a match the following week when their Blackheath League, Division II, match against Army Ordnance Corps Reserves was postponed because the army team were playing in the Charlton Charity Cup.

But they turned out anyway, as the reserve team against Personnel Ordnance College Reserves in a home match at Pound Park in Division IIIA of the Woolwich League.

Charlton won 4-1, and the College complained that they "were rather shabbily treated" with just one Charlton player being a true reserve. The military team were very young and the match report comments "the men were too fast for the boys".

Woolwich Albion "did over" Charlton Athletic Reserves

December 12, 1908

Excitable times as Addicks pour paint on Rotherhithe

The Addicks started the New Year away to Rotherhithe Town in a Lewisham League game, and this time it was a paint pot that the fishmonger toppled onto his opponents as Charlton inflicted on the Town their first home defeat of the season.

According to the Independent, there was a "good crowd of excitable spectators". The excitement seemed to spread to the pitch too with play in the second half "very vigorous" and a couple of the Town players getting a verbal warning from the referee.

Charlton took the lead in the first half after Harry Gritton met a centre from the left-wing and hit the Rotherhithe goalkeeper. The ball rebounded out and Gritton got onto it to put the ball in the net. Charlton held on to the lead in the second half despite losing a player from injury a quarter of an hour before time.

The next Saturday, the Addicks had another eventful afternoon in the Lewisham League with their visitors to Pound Park, Lewisham United, turning up with just six men. They conceded the points but Charlton made up their team with five of their own players and then went on to win the friendly by 5-0.

Later in the month came a bizarre twist on the shortened reserves' away game against St. Mary's Rectory on November 28 the previous year, which Charlton were losing 2-0. In the return match in the Woolwich League, both sides were ordered to play the remaining three minutes of the November game before starting the return. No more goals were scored so St. Mary's were the winners. In the second match, St. Mary's took the lead again but the Addicks then went on to beat them 4-1.

Another victim claimed by the Athletic

January 2, 1909

The Addicks cartoons

Smelly game of fish and a gasworks starts a saga

his was a semi-final match in the Woolwich Cup. In those days,
teams from over the water competed in both cups and leagues
south of the river. New Beckton were a powerful side of the time
and were to go on to win the Woolwich League championship this season.
The fledgling and still relatively unknown Charlton side were very much
the underdogs. But the underdogs were to prove tough opponents and the
tie turned out to be the start of a saga which took almost two months to
resolve, with two replays needed.

The game took place at a neutral venue, the Church Manorway ground
at Plumstead, the home of Pellipar Old Boys. In the first half on a very
wintry day, the Addicks were forced to defend with a strong wind against
them and snow blowing in their faces. But in a breakaway, they won a
penalty and scored. In the second half, the Addicks did the pressing with
the wind now behind them but it was New Beckton who scored the one –
and equalising – goal. The teams played another half hour of extra time.
Neither could score but it appeared that the Addicks finished the fitter. In
the words of the Independent report, "it was plain to see that New
Beckton were far more worn out than the Athletic". Beckton then was a
solid working class area with a gasworks (closed in 1969) – no yuppies or
new housing then. And the New Beckton gas may not have been the
cleanest, as the fishmonger's jibe makes clear, although the side's base was
actually the Manorway Ground, North Woolwich.

It was a long winter for football. The following week the Blackheath
League reported that all its games were cancelled because of the weather.
Among the casualties was the Addicks v. Rotherhithe Invicta match.

Rather a surprise for Becky

February 27, 1909

Soldiers wait as Addicks face unruly Beckton

The cup-tie saga continued through two more games, and near the end of April, the team already through to the final, the Army Service Corps reserve side, were still waiting to know who their opponents were to be.

The first replay took place on Callender's Athletic Ground at Belvedere with a 2d. admission charge. But in the preceding week, New Beckton had been involved in a match with a lot of player trouble, against another prominent Charlton team of those days, Lansdowne.

According to the Independent's football columnist, Corner Flag: "I learn that the game between New Beckton and Lansdowne last Saturday was anything but what it should have been, and the referee found it necessary to bring it to a close before time was up. Of course, this will mean an inquiry, and perhaps suspensions. It does seem a pity that young men cannot play for ninety minutes without losing their temper and bringing discredit upon the game".

But New Beckton appeared to be on better behaviour in the replay. With the game dominated by another strong wind, Charlton had the advantage of the conditions in the first half and went 2-0 up with two goals in the five minutes before the interval. But New Beckton scored thirty minutes into the second half and then five minutes from the end, to bring the tie yet again into extra time. Charlton went ahead again but yet again New Beckton scored five minutes from time.

The result a 3-3 draw and another game – this time again at Church Manorway, Plumstead, admission again 2d. For the winners lay ahead a game at the Manor Ground, Plumstead, the home of Woolwich Arsenal.

To-morrow, New Beckton and Charlton Athletic will meet for the third time in the semi-final of Woolwich Cup

April 24, 1909

Gasworks explode but no final at Woolwich Arsenal

At the third time of asking, the Addicks overcame New Beckton, winning by 2 goals to 1. All the goals came in the first half with Beckton scoring after 15 minutes, but the Addicks coming back strongly to score twice. Although down to ten men early in the second half, after one of their players was injured, the Addicks managed to hold on against what the Independent described as a heavier team.

It also reported a "a great deal of interest" in the match and a large crowd. But so late in the season had the saga gone on, that the final at Woolwich Arsenal's ground had to be held over until next season.

Meanwhile some of the reasons were emerging why Charlton's experiment with a reserve side was to be shortlived. The club obviously had problems getting the numbers for a second team, and matters came to a head in a Woolwich League game against Charlton Villa in January which had to be called off because the Addicks couldn't get enough players together.

In those days, Saturday morning working was the norm and it was an exertion to get home from heavy industrial work and then face a game shortly afterwards.

The fixture was rescheduled for two months later, on Saturday, March 20, but again the Charlton reserves failed to put in an appearance.

The incident infuriated the Villa who commented: "Owing to their inability to get a team out, the Athletic conceded the points. The Villa think this treatment very unsportsmanlike, as they were not notified, and were all on the ground with the ref. This is the second time the same thing has happened".

The end of the semi-finals

April 24, 1909

The Addicks win their first-ever cup trophy

Although the fledgling Charlton team had won five league titles, the delayed Woolwich Cup final gave them their first ever victory in a cup competition. Instead of the grander surrounds of the old Arsenal ground, the final took place in the humbler environment of Creed's Farm, Cemetery Lane, Charlton, with the admission price 3d.

Despite drizzling rain, a crowd of around 2,000 turned out to see Charlton win by 3-0 against the previous holders, the Army Service Corps whose first team were the Army Cup holders. Charlton were one-nil ahead at half-time through 'Razor' Calcutt, and then, after a goalmouth scramble soon after the second half began, Harry Gritton got the ball in the net for the second. Just before time, Calcutt added a third.

Charlton received the cup from the competition's chairman, Alf Myers. It capped off a season, 1908/09, in which they had won every competition they entered: the Woolwich Cup, Lewisham League Division I (after a 2-1 win in a play-off against North Greenwich Amateurs after the teams finished level on points), and Blackheath League Division II.

But the new season saw the end of the club's association with the league in which the club had first started, the Lewisham League. During their three-year stay, they had won all three divisions in succession.

Instead, the team returned to the Woolwich League, the reserve side having been disbanded. They took their place in the top division, Division I, as well as Division I of the Blackheath League (in reality the second division, as there was a senior division). The Blackheath League was the more senior of the two, the Woolwich League (founded 1891) only being revived in 1905/6 after closing down at the end of the 1901/2 season.

Charlton Athletic made "a good haul"

On the warpath – Redpath Brown get double scalping

Two weeks after winning the Woolwich Cup, the Addicks were back in action in the same competition, in the first round of the new season. Their opponents were the Greenwich works team Redpath Brown. Both sides played in the same division of the Blackheath League and both had started the season undefeated.

But it turned out to be a one-sided contest, with Charlton romping home by 4-1 despite several of their leading players being absent. Fred Marshall scored the first at the end of the first half after a weak clearance by the Redpath Brown goalkeeper, to give the Addicks a 1-0 lead. Harry Gritton and 'Razor' Calcutt added two more in the second half before Jack Sudds capped the match by scoring from a free kick 25 years out.

Despite playing in two leagues, Charlton still had vacant Saturdays to fill. With New Beckton pulling out of their Blackheath League game the following Saturday, Charlton played a friendly away to Plumstead Central Hall, winning 4-1. And at the same time, their secretary Harry Hughes was advertising for a friendly on a vacant date on Saturday, December 4.

And on top of that, Charlton had entered another cup competition, the Charlton Charity Cup which had been run since 1904 to raise money for the Hospital Saturday Fund, money much needed for the treatment of the working class people of the district in those pre-National Health Service days. And who should Charlton's opponents be in the first round but Redpath Brown. Charlton were drawn away and this time the result was a 2-2 draw. But Charlton made no mistake in the replay, netting two goals in the first five minutes and running out 5-0 winners. According to the Independent, the game attracted "a very large attendance".

Charlton Athletic "scalped" Redpath Brown

October 30, 1909

Addicks burgle the goals and notch a record victory

Charlton were now developing so rapidly as a team that there was the danger of mismatches. One of their outclassed victims was the Plumstead team, Manor House. The Addicks thumped six past them in a home Woolwich League match – taking the swag as depicted in the cartoon. But just three weeks later an even worse fate was to befall the hapless House. In the second round of the Woolwich Cup, Charlton notched their highest recorded score so far in their short history, 12-2, in another home tie. According to the Independent, "The House were the first to obtain a goal, but Charlton soon got going, and led by 4-2 at the interval. The second moiety was nothing more than a farce, the visitors' defence being pierced on eight occasions". Charlton's scorers were Fred Marshall (4), Albert 'Mosky' Mills (3), Harry Gritton (2), 'Razor' Calcutt, W. 'Chummy' Higgs and Arthur Ellis.

Yet despite the obvious gap in playing ability, both sides competed in the same league, Division I of the Woolwich League.

Meanwhile, the celebration of Charlton winning the previous delayed Woolwich Cup final was not just confined to that game itself. On the night of the following Saturday after the Manor House league game, a social and musical evening was held at the headquarters of the Woolwich Cup competition, the Woolwich Infant pub in Plumstead Road. Besides the cup, the team got gold medals, with the defeated Army Service Corps team getting silver medals. In the words of the Independent: "Midway through the evening... Mr. Alf. C. Myers made the presentations to the players, and musical honours were accorded both the chairman and the Athletic. 'Auld Lang Syne' brought a most successful evening to a close".

Charlton Athletic successfully burgled Manor House

November 13, 1909

Addicks gain supremacy in battle of the Charltons

Christmas Day, 1909, marked one of the most significant dates in the club's early history. A friendly was arranged with Charlton Albion at the latter's home ground at Fossdene Field. Albion were the Charlton team of that era. Founded in 1896, they developed into a very powerful side, and at the time of the encounter were playing in both the London League Division II and the Senior Division of the Blackheath League. Just the previous Saturday, they had lost by just 3-2 to Millwall Reserves away at Millwall.

It was only by overtaking the Albion as the leading side in the area that Charlton were in a position to make the jump into the Football League after the First World War – really as a compensation for Arsenal's departure from Woolwich in 1913. But by the time of the Christmas Day game, Albion were already an ailing outfit with money troubles and their support falling off. Their home from the early days of the century was the Angerstein Lane ground which Charlton Athletic were later to use. In the 1907/8 season, the cash-strapped Albion brought in their powerful rivals Deptford Invicta to share the ground, only to be forced to pass control of it on a lease the following summer and then have to leave it to move to Fossdene Field.

The result of the match was 2-1 to the Addicks. A 'junior' side in the terminology of amateur football of those days had beaten an established 'senior' side. The balance of power in Charlton had changed for good.

The Addicks led 1-0 at half-time through 'Mosky' Mills with Harry Gritton scoring after the break. In the words of the Addicks' own match report, the juniors "sprang a great surprise upon the Albion's supporters".

JUNIORS BEAT SENIORS
Charlton Athletic surprised Charlton Albion

Christmas Day, Saturday, December 25, 1909

North of the river men get a dousing from Addicks

Among the clubs playing with Charlton in Division I of the Woolwich League were two sides from north of the river, both from Silvertown, Silvertown Athletic and Silvertown Rubber Works. By February, there were just two unbeaten teams, the Addicks and Silvertown Athletic who also played in the West Ham League. They clashed in a home encounter and Charlton won by 2-1.

It was, as might be expected, a keen and lively game, and 'Razor' Calcutt put Charlton ahead after half an hour. The 'Town' equalised early in the second half, and then Jack Sudds scored the winner from thirty yards out "with a beautiful shot, which was by far the best goal of the match", according to the report in the Independent. "After this, play was as fast as ever, but very even, and when the final whistle sounded, Charlton were swarming round the visitors' citadel".

Not only were Charlton unbeaten but they had won all six games they had played in the six team league, beating Manor House in the return away fixture by another double-digit score, 10-0.

But the decline of Charlton Albion continued apace. They played a man short in the away London League game at Leyton against Peel Athletic, leading the Independent's columnist, Corner Flag, to comment: "I am very sorry they turned up short, for in addition to the 2s. 6d. per man fine for this sort of thing, it looks bad for a senior club to be short of players".

In their London League match at home to Bronze Athletic, they attracted "barely 20 people" according to Corner Flag. He wondered "how the club manages to exist".

"Doused" by the 'Addicks

February 5, 1910

Addicks supporters called hooligans after cup defeat

Meeting Army teams was a regular occurrence for Charlton in those days, close as they were to one of the major military areas in the country. Although some of the Army teams did play in local leagues, it was mainly in the local cups that they competed against civilian sides.

The second round – and quarter final – of the Charlton Charity Cup saw the Addicks drawn against yet another military team after their Woolwich Cup Final encounter with the Army Service Corps.

This time their opponents were the Army Ordnance Corps Reserves and the away tie involved just a short journey to Woolwich Common. The military men proved too strong as Charlton went down 2-1, despite taking the lead after ten minutes through Arthur Ellis. Their opponents hit back with two goals before the interval and the second half was scoreless.

But the match was more notable for its repercussions, with Corner Flag reporting that in less than 48 hours two "very bad" reports were made about the conduct of the Charlton supporters, one by the referee, Mr. W. Houghton, and the other by the home club itself.

Corner Flag went on: "In fact, if it had not been for the protection afforded by the soldiers, the referee would have been very badly assaulted, violence being attempted all the way from the ground to the dressing room. In addition, the referee was subjected to bad language by the supporters all through the game, and the conduct was generally nothing short of hooliganism".

Meanwhile, Charlton hit back by protesting about the eligibility for the junior competition of some of the Army Ordnance Corps players.

The 'Addick didn't like being "hooked" by the Army Ordnance Corps

February 12, 1910

The sparks fly as Addicks get cup game replayed

The controversial Charlton Charity Cup game against the Army Ordnance Corps had its repercussions. In a long letter to the Independent, the Charlton secretary Harry Hughes queried Corner Flag's version of events. The letter was a little ingenuous in that Harry did not seek to deny the incidence of bad behaviour but to query whether the people concerned were actually Charlton supporters.

The basis of his argument was that the Barrack Field on the Common, where the game took place, was also home to three or four other matches at the same time. So how did Corner Flag, alias Mr. Stanley Hudson, also secretary of the Charity Cup committee and a distinguished local referee, know that the fans behaving badly among the 2,000 to 3,000 fans who watched the game were actually Charlton supporters. Which begged the question as to if they were not Charlton supporters, why should neutrals get so worked up at the referee and the result of the game?

But whatever the logic of this argument, Charlton were on very firm ground indeed in alleging that ineligible players had turned out for the army team. Three of the men were found to have played for the senior level Army Ordnance Corps team in the Kent League whereas the junior team Charlton were supposedly facing competed in the Blackheath League. So the Charity Cup Committee ordered the game to be replayed.

The replay took place on a Tuesday evening before another large crowd – of about 3,000 – and Charlton turned the tables with a 2-0 victory, both goals coming in the second half, from Fred Marshall and 'Razor' Calcutt. With Charlton winning the argument on eligibility of players, the allegations of hooliganism appear not to have been followed up.

The A.O.C. got a rude shock from the 'Addicks

Tuesday, March 22, 1910

Army Service Corps get to detest the whiff of Addick

Charlton's early season opponents in the final of the Woolwich Cup, Army Service Corps, now met them again – this time in this season's semi-final of the cup. The margin of victory was even more decisive with the Addicks romping away to an 8-0 win after being three up at half-time despite facing a strong wind against them.

The growing status of Charlton in the area's football led to what were almost certainly the club's first representative honours. Four players were picked for the Woolwich League side to play Woolwich Arsenal Reserves at the Arsenal ground at Plumstead, Manor Field – Jack Sudds, 'Razor' Calcutt, 'Mosky' Mills, and Fred Marshall.

The full side read: Middleton, Slark (both Plumstead St. John's), Regan (St. Patrick's Hibernians), Peck (Lansdowne), Cunningham (Plumstead St. John's), Sudds (Charlton Athletic), Jecock (Lansdowne), Calcutt (Charlton Athletic), Marshall (Charlton Athletic), Sillet (Charlton Villa), Mills (Charlton Athletic). Reserves: Gee (Bexleyheath), Izzet (Plumstead St. John's), Boyce (Metropolitan Water Board), Buckingham (Ironians).

Ironically, in view of the wealth of the present day Arsenal, the match was in aid of the Arsenal 'Voluntary Fund'. The Arsenal were then in a financial crisis, heralding the move just three years away to Islington. Ironically too, the match was played on Friday, April 1.

The result was a very predictable one, a decisive 5-1 victory for the professional side.

The day afterwards, Charlton clinched the championship of the Blackheath League Division I – that season a division of only five teams – by beating Redpath Brown 2-1 at home.

The A.S.C. can't face 'em now

April 9, 1910

Addicks' cup runneth over, filled time and time again

As with the semi-final of the Woolwich Cup, Charlton again ran into familiar opponents in the final – the same team who had taken them to three games in the semi-final of the previous season's competition, New Beckton. This time Charlton did get their chance to make their debut at Woolwich Arsenal's Manor Field. The game was played on a Monday evening and Charlton ran out comfortable winners.

Peter Ladd opened the scoring after 56 minutes, after a mistake by a Beckton back, with 'Razor' Calcutt adding a second ten minutes later and 'Mosky' Mills putting the result beyond doubt just before the final whistle.

Charlton became the first team to win the cup for a second season running and the Independent reported: "After the match, Mr. Geo. Digby, vice-president of the competition, in a pithy little speech, complimented the victors and presented the cup to them. The Athletic's captain, Mr King, responded. *(This was Bill 'Bodger' King, the side's goalkeeper)*

"Both teams and several friends afterwards adjourned to the headquarters, Woolwich Infant, at the invitation of Host. G. Digby, and had a most enjoyable evening. Members of both teams contributed to an impromptu concert, at which the cup was filled time and time again, and 'Good Luck' wished the victors".

The following week, as winners also of the Woolwich League Division I, Charlton played a League representative team at Pound Park, drawing 2-2. They also made a quick return to Manor Field in the final of the Charlton Charity Cup and there their luck run out. Facing heavy rain and having already played two games that week to complete their season, they went down 2-1 to another military team, Personnel Ordnance College.

Charlton walks off with the Woolwich Cup again

Monday, April 25, 1910

Charlton win the League but aren't promoted

In these modern days, the football structure of the opening years of the last century is a little hard to fathom. The Charlton first team had played and won two leagues in the 1909/10 season but they were only able to compete in both because of the small numbers – five teams in the Blackheath League Division I and six in the Woolwich League Division I.

Their winning the Woolwich League meant they were the overall champions as Division I was the top division. But in the Blackheath League, there was a division above – the Senior Division. Modern logic might dictate that having won Division I, Charlton would be promoted to the Senior Division. But that was a 'senior' amateur league, whereas Charlton were a 'junior' side, so they stayed down.

The close season witnessed the disappearance of the 'senior' team in Charlton, the debt-ridden Albion, who merged with another Charlton team, Lansdowne. Apparently the Lansdowne players formed the majority of the new team, to be called Charlton Amateurs, who were to play with the Addicks in Division I of the Woolwich League, and also in the junior section of the Southern Suburban League.

Meanwhile the Addicks celebrated yet another successful season with a 'concert' supper at the Royal Oak, Charlton Lane, in July. Besides the officials of the club, some forty supporters also attended.

But still in the new season, 1910/11, the team never seemed to have a vacant Saturday, filling in with friendlies when there were not cup or league games. The cartoon depicted Charlton's 4-0 friendly victory over Plumstead Ascension Mission in a match played at East Wickham.

A GREAT EVENT
Charlton Athletic were successful – beating Plumstead Ascension Mission
by 4 goals to nil

September 10, 1910

Rubber men twirl the Addicks out of London cup

Charlton entered a new cup this season – the London Junior Cup. They appeared to have dropped out of the Charlton Charity Cup to undertake the new fixtures. Although the competition was London-wide, it was played in geographical areas up to and including the fourth round.

After coming through games with local rivals Army Service Corps, Woolwich Men's Institute and Braby's Ironworks, Charlton met their nemesis in the sectional final in the shape of Silvertown Rubber Works.

The game took place at North Woolwich and ended in a 2-2 draw. In the replay at Pound Park, Charlton were beaten 4-1 with the 'Rubbers' scoring four in the first half. Arthur Ellis got one back for Charlton in the second. This was Charlton's first defeat of the season.

The previous winners of the cup were Charlton's old rivals, Redpath Brown, yet surprisingly Redpath Brown were going through a crisis at this time and temporarily disbanded.

A few weeks earlier, the Addicks had run into trouble in a home Blackheath League game with Price's Athletic, which they won 3-2, the winner coming from a penalty kick. The referee sent off the Charlton centre-half (un-named) and the Price's centre forward for "ungentlemanly conduct".

On the same afternoon, in another Blackheath League match, the game between Dartmouth Athletic and Royal Victoria had to be suspended for 16 minutes because of both player and crowd trouble. The Independent's Corner Flag commented: "It is not only bad for the clubs but bad for the competition in which they play".

The Rubber Man gave the Haddick (Charlton Athletic) a surprise

December 10, 1910

ASC suffer that fishy smell again as the goals pile in

O f all the Army teams in the Woolwich area, the Army Service Corps must have been more sick of the sight of Charlton Athletic than any other. Having lost the delayed Woolwich Cup final (1908/9) last season, and then crashing to them by 8-0 in that season's Woolwich Cup semi-finals, they also had gone down by 6-0 at home earlier this season in October in the London Junior Cup. They now faced the civilians in the second round of the Woolwich Cup at Pound Park.

The result was a small improvement – this time just 5-0. The coming Christmas seemed to put a brake on the attendance. The match report stated: "The crowd was not so large as usual, but the faithful saw the 'Boys' show something like their best form, and it is hoped that now all the players are eligible, the team will settle down to their best form".

In those days, Charlton indulged in Christmas period games with a vengeance. No daylong Christmas television programmes then or the King's Speech at 3p.m. In an era when leisure was sparse, the Christmas days were a chance to get a little more precious open air. The Addicks' football schedule was three games in four days.

On Christmas Eve, Saturday, December 24, Charlton were due to meet Catford Southend Reserves at home in the Blackheath League but this had to be called off because the Catford reserves were still in the London Junior Cup. On Boxing Day, Monday, December 26, Charlton arranged a friendly at home against West Ham Thursday and won 5-1. On Tuesday, December 27, they played a 'weak team' in a friendly against Woolwich Southern Star but still won 1-0. But according to the club "the matches during the holidays were not so well supported as was expected".

The 'Addicks were too strong for the Army Service Corps

December 17, 1910

The Addicks cartoons

Same game but Athletic and Amateurs beg to differ

The new amalgamated team Charlton Amateurs came up against the Addicks in a Woolwich League match at their home ground, Fossdene Field, but failed to check their rivals' success, going down 2-0. The local rivalry encouraged a big crowd although the conditions were foggy and frosty, with the pitch frozen. The Amateurs did not help themselves by playing only ten men for the first 15 minutes, either one or several of their players arriving late because of weather hold-ups.

Both teams sent in match reports to the Independent which gave rather different accounts of the game. According to the Athletic report, they pressed from the kick-off and were soon two up. "The Athletic were content to hold the lead obtained, and for the rest of the game took things in an easy way, playing four half-backs. This was the best plan, considering the state of the ground and future engagements".

According to the Amateurs, end-to-end play ensued after they got their eleventh man and they had the better of the exchanges up to half-time, "but try as they could, they could not score". The Amateurs described play in the second half as "very evenly contested".

Away from the opinions, the facts were that Arthur Ellis scored the opening goal while the Amateurs had only ten men, and Johnny Mitchell scored from a penalty kick midway through the first half.

Charlton had faced the problem of depleted opponents a fortnight earlier as well, in another Woolwich League game, with a very different outcome. They travelled to Woolwich Barracks to play the 49 Brigade R.F.A. but the soldiers refused to play because they could not raise a full team and also turned down playing a friendly using unregistered players.

The 'Addicks were too strong for the Amateurs

January 14, 1911

Fishmonger rides cable 'racer' over the heavies

The Woolwich Cup was proving a very good competition for Charlton and, after winning the trophy for two seasons running, they now dispatched one of the strongest works sides in the area, Callender's Athletic, by 1-0 in the semi-final at Church Manorway, Plumstead.

According to the Charlton match report in the Independent: "The game was contested keenly throughout, both teams attacking in turn, with Charlton ever dangerous when near goal, but showing very poor shooting ability. Callender's were much the heavier side and played good football".

Besides military teams, works teams were very much part of local football in this era. In addition to Callender's, Charlton's works opponents in their early years included teams such as Silvertown Rubber Works, Braby's Ironworks, East Greenwich Gasworks, Price's Athletic, and Johnson and Phillips, as well as the stricken Redpath Brown.

A fortnight later, victory in their Blackheath League game against Braby's Ironworks gave Charlton the championship of Division I for the second year running. The league's Dewar Shield was clinched in an away match with Braby's at Lee, Charlton winning 5-0 in a game affected by the weather in the form of a very strong wind.

It was their 13th consecutive victory in cup and league games, proof of just what a force the team were becoming in this south of the Thames area and also against teams just north of the river.

It also completed a hat-trick of Blackheath League wins, the Addicks having taken the Division II title in 1908/9, although this season was to be their last season in the competition.

Charlton Athletic "came out on top" of Callender's

March 11, 1911

Easter brings cup hat-trick and league championship

E aster 1911 saw Charlton wrap up the championship of the Woolwich League in their closing game in the competition – a 2-1 home win on the Saturday against Charlton Amateurs. Then, on Easter Monday, they clinched a hat-trick of Woolwich Cup victories, beating the North Woolwich side Claremont 2-1 in the final at Manorway Ground, North Woolwich. According to the cup match report, "a battle royal was seen, the play at times being of quite a high standard". 'Mosky' Mills scored what were described as "two brilliant goals".

In contrast, the Amateurs game "was a somewhat tame affair. Possibly the players held a bit in reserve for Monday". The cartoon of Charlton's fine Easter haul does not make it clear which team the fishmonger is hauling up but we do know the Amateurs played in hoops as did their Albion predecessors, and Claremont wore stripes – so it looks like Claremont.

Just two games over a holiday period was almost light work for the Addicks but Good Friday had seen the involvement of two players in a representative side. In aid of the Woolwich League's trophy fund, a match was held for the first time between league teams North of the River and South of the River. The south team included Arthur Ellis and 'Razor' Calcutt and the game was played at 11.30a.m. at the ground of Silvertown Rubber Works. The south team met at the Woolwich Free Ferry at 10.30a.m. for their journey across the river. They were defeated 5-2.

Charlton's last-ever game in the Blackheath League saw them draw 1-1 away to Price's at Belvedere the next Saturday, and they ended the season a week later by beating a rest of the Woolwich League team 1-0 at Pound Park, Eddie Marshall scoring a few minutes from the end.

The Athletic made a fine holiday haul

Easter, Sat, April 15, & Mon, April 17,1911

The Addicks enter London suburbia and travel west

For some reason, it was to be almost a year before the Kentish Independent's cartoonist turned his attentions once again to Charlton. By then eventful progress had been made, with the club moving up in status to play in the junior section of the powerful Southern Suburban League although retaining their place in the Woolwich League.

This move into a far wider area of London suburbia brought a new range of opponents to Charlton, including the reserve sides of Bromley (Amateur Cup winners in 1911), Dulwich Hamlet and Sutton United.

But Charlton, playing in what was termed the First Division (Eastern Section), were easily able to step up on to this level. By the time Dulwich Hamlet Reserves visited Pound Park near the end of March, they were the only Southern Suburban team to have beaten the Addicks, winning 2-1 in the first game at Dulwich on the Saturday before Christmas 1911.

According to the return match report: "The wretched weather spoilt what would have been one of the tit-bits of the season when Dulwich Hamlet sent over a very powerful reserve team to battle for Southern Suburban League points, but the few spectators who braved the elements saw a splendidly-contested game from the kick-off to the finish".

Charlton had to play with ten men in the second half after Sammy Mew injured an ankle and were missing three regular first-team players but still managed to win 1-0 with a goal from Tommy Beldham.

The season saw the first Charlton players to be recognised by the London Football Association, Bob Smith and 'Mosky' Mills playing in the London Juniors team against Middlesex Juniors at Wealdstone FC in January and then against the West End Association the following month.

Dulwich Hamlet saw a ghost last Saturday

March 23, 1912

Sad Easter – the passing away of John Garrett

As usual, Charlton had a crowded Easter programme with three games in four days. But on the Monday before the holiday began, the Addicks lost one of their founding fathers – their president John Garrett. He died at his home at 142 West Street (now Westmoor Street) at the age of 78. Up to his death, he had run his shipbreaking and timber yard at Sunderland Wharf, just to the west of where the modern Thames Barrier building stands. He had guided the boys who formed Charlton in 1905, and had succeeded Harry Wells, the first president.

The funeral took place on the Easter Saturday at Charlton Cemetery. John had been a pillar of the riverside community where Charlton were founded, and not just the Charlton Athletic club but many others paid their respects, including the Crown Bowling Club, the Anchor and Hope Rowing Club and the Jolly Boys' Slate Club. According to the Independent report, "the floral tributes were numerous and beautiful".

During the holiday games, the Charlton players wore crepe armlets as a mark of respect. On Good Friday, they beat Crawford's United in a friendly at Fossdene Field by 3-0, with goals from Fred Marshall, Tommy Beldham and Jack Sudds. On the Saturday afternoon, they met their local rivals Charlton Amateurs in the Southern Suburban League before 800 spectators, again away at Fossdene Field. After playing "very quietly" in the first half, they laid siege in the second to the Amateurs' goal. Harry Gritton scored after 65 minutes from a Beldham cross to take the points. But on Easter Monday, in a tie to decide the Woolwich League championship, the Addicks went down 1-0 at Pound Park to Claremont who thus deprived the Addicks of a hat-trick of league titles.

The "'Addicks" were just a little too strong for the Amateurs

Easter Saturday, April 6, 1912

Addicks beat Surrey rivals to take the Eastern title

Despite their failure to clinch the Woolwich League title, Charlton topped the Eastern section of the much more powerful Southern Suburban League. Their last opponents were the winners of the Surrey Junior Cup, Beddington Corner.

The game was played at home at Pound Park and the Addicks gained a decisive victory by 3-0, with "A. Mitchell giving a fine display at right-half, as did C. Ladd at inside left".

Their Southern Suburban League record read: Played 20, Won 19, Drawn 0, Lost 1, Points 38, Goals for 83, Goals against 8. The only defeat had been the away game against Dulwich Hamlet Reserves. It was an impressive achievement indeed for a side who had taken such a step upwards in junior London football. The League First Division also had a Western Section so Charlton's triumph meant they now had to play the Western champions Summerstown II, for the overall championship.

The year of 1912 is memorable in history for one thing above all - the sinking of the Titanic, and all around the country fundraising exercises were held to help the victims of the disaster.

The Woolwich League decided to join in, and as a fundraiser to repeat its successful innovation of a North of the River versus South of the River match. Again two Charlton players were chosen for the South team, Tommy Beldham and 'Mosky' Mills, in addition to another player who was to figure prominently in Charlton's early history, Alfred 'Scotty' Kingsley, then of Blackheath St. John's. The game eventually took place in May at Woolwich Arsenal's Manor Ground, and ended in a 2-2 draw, with both Mills and Kingsley singled out for their performances.

Ever been 'ad?

April 20, 1912

League triumph marred as Bob Smith breaks leg

Charlton went on to take the Southern Suburban League First Division title – the Dewar Challenge Shield – by beating Summerstown II 5-1 in a game played on the Wimbledon Borough FC ground at Copper Mill Lane, Tooting. But the triumph was marred by a serious injury to the club's right back Bob Smith, who broke his leg after just 20 minutes play. According to the report of the match: "At that time there was no score, but Charlton rose to their task manfully, played brilliant football, and ran out victors... J. Mitchell played a great game at back, as did A. Mills forward".

Bob was taken to St. James's Infirmary, Wandsworth, and kept in hospital for many weeks. The injury meant more than just a loss on the playing field but the player also suffering "loss of salary and employment". To help him and his financially stricken family, the club set about organising a benefit concert which was to take place successfully in June.

On the following Tuesday evening, the Addicks met their old rivals, Army Service Corps Reserves, in the final of the Charlton Charity Cup, at the Woolwich Arsenal ground, with threepence (1¼ modern pennies) the price of admission. Having lost in the final two seasons ago, Charlton won the trophy for the first time with a 2-0 victory, both goals coming from Fred Marshall, the first from a penalty for handball.

Off the playing field, the result was a little different. The specific aim of the Charity Cup was to raise money for the local Hospital Saturday Fund. But the Tuesday night date was forced upon the organisers because of a fixture pile-up. The gate was low and, as a fundraising exercise, the fixture was "a complete failure".

The "Addicks" finished strongly with two fine catches

Saturday, April 27, & Tuesday, April 30, 1912

Smart new handbook starts off Addicks' season

Charlton completed in devastating style the first match of their seventh season in league competition, defeating the Croydon A team 10-0 at Pound Park in the First Division of the Southern Suburban League. According to the match report "a good crowd was present, and showed delight at the form of the locals". The game was marked by a fine display from Eddie Marshall at centre half and hat-tricks for Albert Mitchell and 'Mosky' Mills.

The first mention of a club handbook also came in the Kentish Independent where the Corner Flag column reported:

"I am indebted to Mr E. Heath, the hon. secretary of Charlton Athletic, for a copy of the club's handbook. This is one of the smartest little works I have seen from a junior club. The team has no less than twenty-four league games, and as they are also competing in the London Junior, Woolwich and Charlton Charity Cups, they have a busy time before them. I notice that they did not commence league football until season 1906-7, and since then have won no less than fourteen competitions. This is a record to be proud of".

No copies of that handbook appear to have survived but Eddie Heath, who had combined his secretaryship of the Woolwich League with that of Charlton Athletic in 1910, was a busy man, bringing out the league handbook a few weeks later and receiving yet more praise from Corner Flag.

"Nothing for the good of the league seems to have been forgotten. Last year's balance sheet shows an income of over £46, and after meeting all expenses a balance is carried forward. The league consists of four divisions and thirty-four clubs".

Croydon A was badly upset by the Charlton 'Addicks

September 7, 1912

Fireworks blitz in Peckham as the big scores pile up

Another double digit victory took place when Charlton journeyed to Peckham to play Choumert FC in the Southern Suburban League. This time the score was 10-1. Charlton had so far won every game in all competitions they had played in the season, and all by decisive scores.

The list of the other victims read: Callender's Athletic beaten 8-0 at Pound Park in a Woolwich League match, Army Ordnance Department beaten away 4-1 in the Woolwich League, Dartmouth Athletic beaten at home in the Charlton Charity Cup by 7-0, Callender's beaten too in the Woolwich Cup, this time away by 6-1, Albany Invicta beaten in the Southern Suburban League away at Camberwell by 8-0, and Bostall Heath beaten 5-0 at home in the Woolwich Cup. Add to that a three goal victory in an away friendly against Blackheath St. John's.

Among the goalscorers were Johnny Mitchell and his brother Albert who between them got five of the goals against Callender's in the Woolwich Cup, Johnny scoring a hat-trick. Then the brothers repeated exactly the same five goal feat together in the game against Albany Invicta. 'Mosky' Mills was also hitting the net regularly for the soaraway Addicks. Meanwhile Eddie Marshall was bolting the defence together with excellent displays at centre half.

After all that, it was down to earth the following week after the Choumert victory with a 2-2 draw at Pound Park in the Southern Suburban League against Catford Excelsior. The draw was all the more disappointing because Charlton went two-up but the match report adds they "were inclined to take matters easily on securing a two-goal lead".

Last Saturday, the 'Addicks had their November celebrations

November 2, 1912

Lino men are completely nailed down by Addicks

This was Charlton's third season in the London Junior Cup and on their performances they looked potential winners, but it was a cup that somehow always eluded them. In this season's third round, Charlton were drawn at home to the amusingly named Linoleum Rangers – a team from Greenwich Linoworks, playing in the Blackheath League.

Although the lino men were reported to have paid "special attention to their training for this game", the result was another decisive victory by 6-0. According to the match report "the visitors were good sportsmen, and were triers to the end, but gave a feeble display in front of goal".

The game was notable in Charlton's early history for what certainly appears to have been the debut of Alfred 'Scotty' Kingsley who was to have a major impact in the club's rapid rise after the Great War. He had been playing for Blackheath St. John's although we have no record of how the switch came about. He evidently had a fine debut. The match report stated: "The forwards, well led by F. Marshall, were splendid, the two wingers, A. Mills and A. Kingsley, being too fast for their opponents".

The next week the club had another Southern Suburban League tussle with Catford Excelsior, the only team so far this season to deny them victory. The Excelsior team actually played at Mottingham and the ground obviously was not to the Addicks' liking, with their match report commenting: "The homesters' ground was not of the billiard table type, and suited their heavy players, but Charlton set about their task with great spirit, and after a hard-fought game, retired victors to the tune of 1-0. The club are to be congratulated upon their victory as not many visitors will conquer at Mottingham".

The 'Addicks quickly laid down the lino

November 16, 1912

Amateurs confounded twice more by Addicks

The next round of the London Junior Cup saw the Addicks drawn against their local rivals Charlton Amateurs, away at Fossdene Field, Charlton. The Amateurs had yet to beat the Addicks, and nor had their predecessors, Charlton Albion, in the solitary match played between the two sides on Christmas Day, 1909. This time, there was real spice to the match as both teams were undefeated so far, the Amateurs playing in the Southern Suburban League and the Blackheath League.

Some 800 people attended, and the Addicks triumphed yet again, by 2-1. Fred Marshall put them ahead in the first half, but Chaplin equalised in the second for the Amateurs (now playing in stripes) from a penalty for handball, who then lost the tie to a fine shot by Albert Mitchell.

Both sides sent in their match reports. The Athletic commented: "Both teams indulged in the good old-fashioned shoulder charge, with the greatest of gusto, and never descending to dirty or unclean play". According to the Amateurs, their undoing "was their style of play in the first half, which did not suit the occasion, for the robust methods of the visitors completely upset their game". They were to meet again in a Southern Suburban game on Christmas Day morning at Fossdene Field, in a match played "under the most deplorable conditions". Still the Amateurs could not dent their rivals' success, going down by 4-1.

In the first game of 1913, the Addicks again failed in the London Junior Cup, going out for the second season running to Cubitt Town, in a 5th round tie played away at Millwall. Charlton lost 2-1 with the goals coming in the second half. After Cubitt Town went ahead, Albert Mitchell equalised, only for the Addicks to concede again.

The Charlton Amateurs were haunted by the 'Addicks

December 7, 1912

The Addicks cartoons

Valiant league double a foretaste of the future

The Southern Suburban League was proving a fruitful new home for the Addicks. They topped the Division 1 Eastern Section yet again in their second season in the league and then won the championship play-off again.

This time, their opponents were Carshalton who were crushed by 4-0. The fishmonger is depicted as a knight, an ominous foretaste of what was to come 50 years later when Charlton, in attempting to ditch their Addicks and then Robins nicknames, tried to call themselves the Valiants – a very unsuccessful exercise but which nevertheless left the club with the legacy of the sword symbol.

Obviously the cartoonist had no foresight of this – just as he could never have guessed what the S.S. initials were to come to symbolise. The match was played at the Angerstein Lane ground in East Greenwich, the home of Deptford Invicta and the former home of the defunct Charlton Albion club. Next season, it was to be the Addicks' new home.

The Addicks were in command throughout despite a strong wind making play difficult. Johnny Mitchell scored a hat-trick and Herbert Franklin scored the other goal. Runners-up in the Eastern Section were local rivals Charlton Amateurs who also won the Blackheath League Division I (now the top division of that league).

The Addicks had clinched a league double by winning the Woolwich League for the third time in their short history. They made sure of the title in the final league match of the season, beating Army Ordnance Department by 6-0, Johnny Mitchell getting a hat-trick. Peter Ladd with two goals and Eddie Marshall were the other scorers.

Still S.S. Champions

April 26, 1913

The Addicks cartoons

Losing the cup to the Riding Establishment

This was the most splendid Addicks cartoon our unknown artist drew in this pre-First World War era – symbolising both the Addick nickname the club carried and the famous Woolwich military area close to which the club grew up. Suitably adapted, it would surely make a splendid new badge for Charlton, retaining the sword image but getting away from the plain dullness of the modern badge.

Yet the match in question was actually a defeat for the Addicks. It was the final of the Charlton Charity Cup and played on a Monday evening with a 5.15p.m. kick-off at the Woolwich Arsenal ground. Their opponents were the military team the Riding Establishment, Royal Artillery.

The riding men were evidently pretty good on their feet too, for they beat the Addicks 3-1. Charlton went ahead in the first half when from a free-kick close by the corner flag, 'Mosky' Mills swerved the ball into the net without any other player touching it. But the Riding Establishment got two back before the interval, and then got their third in the final minutes of the game.

But in a crowded end-of-season fixture list, the Addicks got their revenge just two days later, on the Wednesday evening. The two teams met again in the final of the Woolwich Cup at the Angerstein ground in East Greenwich. In pouring rain and mudbath conditions, the Addicks won 3-0. According to the match report: "Starting with the toil of grime upon them, the Charltonians ...soon added some of the grime of Mother Earth".

'Mosky' Mills headed home in the first half, and Albert Mitchell and Fred Marshall scored in the second.

The Riding Establishment R.A. snatched the cup from Charlton Athletic

Monday, April 28, 1913

Addicks become a 'senior' team as Arsenal depart

T he 1913/14 season was a highly significant one for Charlton Athletic, a team still less than a decade old. The club moved up from 'junior' amateur status to 'senior', a distinction hard to comprehend in the modern era when even the long-rooted distinction between amateur and professional football has almost entirely disappeared. What it meant was the club moved up to the senior section of the Southern Suburban League and entered Division I of the London League, a very powerful league at that time whose top division (Premier Division, Professional Section) comprised reserve sides of Football League clubs.

They also now entered the London Senior Cup and the Kent Senior Cup. And they moved to a new ground, the Angerstein Lane ground in East Greenwich, which they shared with the Deptford Invicta club. The ground, once the home of the defunct Charlton Albion, was described as "one minute from the Angerstein Hotel".

But what the close season had also seen was the move of the Woolwich Arsenal club to Islington, a move that was to pave the way for the new 'senior' Charlton to move quickly up the ranks of the football ladder to take their place as the Football League club of the Woolwich area.

The Addicks kicked off their first senior season at their new ground in a Southern Suburban fixture against the first team of the Army Ordnance Corps. Before some 500 supporters, they won by 5-1. AOC went ahead in the first half only for 'Scotty' Kingsley to equalise and then Harry Saywood to score twice before the interval. 'Mosky' Mills added two more in the second. According to the match report: "The team as a whole played splendid football and should make their mark in senior circles".

The 'Addicks gave the A.O.C. a sudden fright

September 6, 1913

Surprise Addicks raise the haddock standard high

The Addicks hit the ground running, to use modern phraseology, in their new 'senior' existence, and their 5-0 home beating of West Norwood in the Southern Suburban League made it two wins out of two in this league, and a win and a draw in their two London League games so far.

What was pleasing was another large crowd, for senior status meant a large rise in costs for the Addicks. But compared to Pound Park, it was much easier to collect admission payments at the all-enclosed Angerstein ground. For this season, they were set at 3d (about 1¼ pence) for adults and 1d (about ⅕ pence) for 'boys' (no mention of girls!) with an extra unspecified charge for the 'enclosure'.

Season tickets were on sale for what appears to be the first time in the Addicks' history. They were priced at 4s (20 pence) while for another shilling, a seat was "provided in the enclosure".

Not everyone had anticipated that the Addicks would make their step up in status so easily. According to the Independent's Corner Flag column: "The success of the Charlton Athletic team is one of the surprises in the district".

Charlton also formed a 'B' reserve team for this season to take part in junior competitions but ran into problems finding a ground, so could not enter a league. The team instead were to compete in junior cup competitions and friendlies.

Meanwhile, the old Arsenal ground at Plumstead had acquired a new tenant, a newly-formed 'Woolwich' club who were accepted to play in the Kent League and whose ambition was certainly Football League status.

The 'Addicks were much above Norwood last Saturday

September 27, 1913

'Junior Haddocks' get a Heathen roasting

The new B team started their 'friendly' existence in promising fashion with a 1-1 draw in their first game, away to Linoleum Rangers at Blackheath Lane, "considering it was their first time out and being mostly strangers to each other". Then, after an away victory 3-2 against Western Electric at Gibson's Farm, Welling, they crashed 4-0 away to Bostall Heath at Cavey's Meadow, Plumstead.

There was no home game that day as the first team, now dubbed the 'A' team, were away to Wealdstone in the London League, so supporters wanting to make the shorter journey to Cavey's Meadow were advised to "take the tram car to Bostall Lane". The B team were one down at the interval and according to the Bostall side's match report: "In the second moiety, the homesters' defence was a rare stumbling block for the 'Junior Haddocks' attack". The cartoon with its Heathen pun is certainly a reflection of the far less racially aware times of this faraway era.

At Wealdstone, the first team continued their unbeaten run with a 1-0 victory. So far, all their London League games had been away, and they had notched five points out of six in the new league (wins counting for two points).

According to the Independent's Corner Flag: "Mr Heath, the club secretary, told me months ago that the question of his club becoming seniors needed earnest consideration, but now the step has been taken, the players and committee are proving themselves to be men of sound judgement". The team, he added, "are playing in such a convincing style that, to my knowledge, they are beginning to attract the attention of those well advanced in the higher circles of the game".

Bostall Heathens enjoyed the young 'Addicks

October 4, 1913

Fair weather fans as rain grounds Park's star runner

The Addicks fans of those days appeared to be 'fair weather fans' for the excellent attendances at the Angerstein ground came to a brief halt for the visit of the Finchley-based club, Tufnell Park, a very powerful side of the day.

The cause was a very wet day in South London. According to the Charlton match report: "Rain poured down from start to finish, and in consequence, very few spectators appeared to witness the game".

The Corner Flag column in the Independent was now commenting regularly on the new senior team and it described the scenario like this: "Half-an-hour before the advertised kick-off (3.15p.m.), the pitch at Angerstein Lane, Charlton, looked as miserable as possible. The water laid about in pools, and everything was wringing wet when the two teams, Charlton Athletic and Tufnell Park, arrived to play their London League game, but financially the day was a dead loss for the local team".

On the field though, it was success again with Charlton beating Tufnell Park 4-1. They were 2-1 up at the interval with goals from Peter Ladd and Harry Saywood, and Saywood and Albert Mitchell added two more in the second half. "The visitors were a fine team, and included the famous runner (A. Applegarth) amongst their forwards but the heavy ground prevented much running", according to the Charlton report.

The B team, doomed to play almost all their games away, had their game against Callender's at Belvedere cancelled because of the weather.

The following week the first team made their debut in the London Senior Cup in a second round tie at Angerstein Lane, beating the London County Council Tramways team 7-0 before "a large crowd".

Tufnell Park caught it from the Charlton 'Addicks

October 11, 1913

Journey into sleepy Kent proves a travel saga

S enior status meant a big increase in the geographical area the Addicks traversed. Apart from travelling to faraway North London places such as Wealdstone, they also now made inroads into Kent with their entry into the Kent Senior Cup.

And certainly their first opponents in the Kent Senior Cup were far removed in environment from the busy Woolwich area the Addicks had grown up in. Snodland was then a rural area to the south of the Medway towns but it boasted a good football team.

The Addicks entered the competition in the second qualifying round and they drew Snodland Town away. The tie was to prove a bit of a travel saga.

The team and their supporters planned to leave Charlton station by train at 1.04p.m. and the supporters were reminded that 'cheap tickets' could be had at the station.

Just as now, the railways in those days were fragmented into many small companies and evidently the result was very much the same. Due to "a disorganised train service", according to the Addicks, they were an hour late in reaching Snodland. But a late start was made "before a big attendance" and Charlton were 4-1 up at half-time. Snodland got another one back in the second half but by then the late afternoon was so dark that the game had to be abandoned and was replayed three weeks later.

This time, the sad but wiser Addicks made the visit by motor bus, leaving the Victoria pub at 12 noon. Before what was described as a "record gate" with over 100 Charlton supporters present, "Charlton had the home team beaten at all points" and won 2-0.

The 'Addicks woke up (S)nodland

November 15, 1913

Charlton far from 'appy as cup tie venue is switched

Hampstead was another of the new places and teams Charlton encountered this season, and in a close struggle at the Angerstein ground, the Addicks held out for a 1-0 victory, Harry Saywood scoring in the second half with a drive that rebounded from the underside of the crossbar into the net.

Nicknamed 'Appy 'Ampstead by the cartoonist, and depicted by a man playing a concertina, the North London suburb certainly appeared to have a different social image in those days.

Charlton's ground sharing with Deptford Invicta seemed to be working for league games, but cup-ties began to impose a headache. In the fourth round of the London Senior Cup, the Addicks were drawn to play Old Kingstonians at home. But the Angerstein ground was not available for the tie on Saturday, November 29.

The Addicks attempted to postpone the match by a fortnight but Old Kingstonians were having none of that, so the tie was switched to Kingston, and again the journey was by motor bus, the departure time 12.30p.m. at the Victoria on the corner of East Street/Woolwich Road.

The game also turned out disastrously. With Charlton winning 2-1 with a quarter of the game gone, their back Herbert Owen was injured and could not resume. Charlton held out until half-time, but Old Kingstonians scored four in the second half for a 5-2 victory.

The B team playing in the Kent Junior Cup beat the so far undefeated Charlton Amateurs 3-2 in a second round tie but were disqualified for an unreported reason. They also competed in the London Junior Cup but went out by losing 2-1 to Storer's Athletic at Millwall in the second round.

'Appy 'Ampstead dropped into it at Charlton

November 22, 1913

The Ilford dry plates are hauled in dripping wet

Ilford films to older generations were the films for cameras, long before the advent in the UK of Kodak, Fuji etc. So when Ilford came to visit Angerstein Lane for a London League game, the cartoonist could not resist the inevitable allusion.

It was a game the Charlton team were up for, and after a strong start by Ilford, they pushed them back "as the result of some strong tackling by the Charlton backs" and then proceeded to dominate, according to the match report. Herbert Owen was one of the backs and had recovered from the injury sustained against Old Kingstonians which had initially looked likely to keep him out for a lengthy time.

All three goals came before the interval, 'Scotty' Kingsley opening the scoring, then H. Spreadbury on his debut scored twice.

According to the report: "The second half needs little description, being practically a duel between the Charlton attack and Ilford's defence". But no further goals were scored.

The B team were also playing strongly and obviously had a younger profile than the A team as they were frequently referred to as the Young Addicks or Young Reds.

They also took the place of the senior side in the local charity competition, the Charlton Charity Cup, and were meeting opponents of the level the first team were playing just a season previously.

In the first round, they played the 31st Battery R.F.A. team on Woolwich Common and beat them 5-0.

The military men of those days were certainly civilised as, after their heavy defeat, they "entertained Charlton to tea".

Charlton Athletic made a wonderful catch last Saturday

December 6, 1913

The Addicks cartoons

Commos make a Christmas pud out of the fishmonger

Army Service Corps, nicknamed the Commos, had long been close rivals of the Addicks, although it was their reserve side the Addicks had previously faced. Now in the Southern Suburban League's Senior Division, they faced the first team of the ASC.

According to the club notice of the game: "Tomorrow should be a red-letter day at Angerstein Lane, for the club will entertain dear friends and rivals, the Army Service Corps, under the auspices of the Southern Suburban League".

This was a game Corner Flag also managed to attend and he reported ... "the Athletic turned out sharp to time looking very fit, and particularly smart in their bright red shirts".

But their fitness was not enough to stop them going down to their first league defeat of the season in a match described as well attended by supporters of both sides.

The match "started at racing speed, and the ball was quickly taken from end to end". In a goalmouth scramble, the soldiers got the ball into the net for a goal and were 1-0 up at the interval. In the second half, ASC scored from a penalty but Charlton got a goal back almost immediately through 'Mosky' Mills which the soldiers disputed as offside. But the Addicks but could not penetrate again a very good ASC defence and went down 2-1.

As always, the Addicks planned a busy holiday programme with three games in three days, starting with a Christmas Day friendly at home against local team Crawford's United. But the fixture had to be postponed as Deptford Invicta were using the Angerstein ground.

The A.S.C. conjured with Charlton Athletic

December 20, 1913

Holiday spirit takes toll of the Christmas games

Charlton's first meeting with their co-tenants at Angerstein Lane, Deptford Invicta, in the Southern Suburban League, turned out to be a strange affair, and one not fully explained in the Kentish Independent reports of the holiday games. Invicta were a powerful team of the time and it should have been an important and significant game.

The game took place on the Saturday of Christmas week and according to the Corner Flag column: "The meeting of these two teams was expected to produce a regular battle royal. But the spectators were sadly disappointed. In the first place, Deptford were short of players; secondly full time was not played; and thirdly there was no life or dash in the game".

Charlton won 4-0 and the club's own report commented: "The players appeared to take things in holiday spirit, and, doubtless, neither team gave of their best, although the issue was never in doubt". The report made no reference to the fact that Deptford were somehow short of players.

Whether Deptford – the Invicta horse in the cartoon – played short of a full eleven or simply called up reserves was not stated in the Independent. But on Christmas Day, Invicta had been unable to field a full team against Cray Wanderers who were themselves short of players.

It was bizarre stuff for teams competing in senior amateur football.

On Boxing Day, the Addicks B team had been in action at Angerstein Lane, against a Woolwich League XI, drawing 1-1. Again, the Christmas period seemed to have a less than dynamic effect on the players with the club's report stating: "The Young Reds did not appear to take the game seriously, as they missed chances galore, and the goal scored by G. Farrer was suspiciously near offside".

The 'Addicks made the old hoss go

December 27, 1913

It's alas, poor Hamlet, as Addicks show true form

Dulwich Hamlet Reserves were Charlton's first opponents of what was to turn out to be the ominous year of 1914. They met in a Southern Suburban League match at Angerstein Lane "before a good gathering" according to the match report.

The game proved to be very different indeed to what looked like the farcical encounter with Deptford Invicta.

Corner Flag in the Kentish Independent commented: "Whatever impression was formed of Charlton Athletic when they played at home against Deptford Invicta during the holiday, there was no nonsense when they entertained Dulwich Hamlet, at Angerstein Lane, last week; in fact, except for the colours one would never have believed the team to consist of the same players.

"From the kick-off the Athletic were out to win, and they did so by 2 good goals to none.

"It was a capital display, Dulwich never having a chance to settle down. Charlton, taking advantage of every opening, showed their spectators that when on their mettle they can play sound football".

'Scotty' Kingsley was noted in the match report as "a source of trouble to the visitors with his long-range shooting".

But more evidence of some of the chaotic organisation of football in this era came the next week.

The London League game at Barking was cancelled for what were described as "unforeseen circumstances".

The B team, however, had a rare home game at Angerstein Lane and beat South Woolwich by 6-2.

The 'Addicks "dropped" in on Dulwich Hamlet

January 3, 1914

Addicker fishmonger in a battle with the shrimps

T he first round proper of the Kent Senior Cup saw Charlton drawn away against the semi-professional Gravesend United, then in the Kent League and based at the Central Avenue Ground. The United team, founded in 1893, was the forerunner of the present Gravesend and Northfleet, merging with the Northfleet United club in 1946. They boasted the nickname of the Shrimpers.

The Charlton team met at Charlton station at 1p.m. for the journey and evidently a good number of fans went with them. According to the match report: "Charlton supporters made themselves heard in no uncertain fashion in the crowd of a thousand strong that fringed the enclosure".

Charlton Athletic were still an unknown quantity at this level of football, and word of their winning runs in their new senior leagues did not seem to have gotten through to the Shrimpers, one of the favourites for the title of the powerful Kent League. The Shrimpers started the game in relaxed fashion but soon realised they had a game on their hands.

Commented Corner Flag: "If the truth is spoken, it may safely be said that Charlton Athletic were not looked on as very serious opponents, but from the time the ball was in motion until the last blast on the whistle Gravesend had to fight their hardest to save the game". The Addicks surprised Gravesend in the opening minutes when, after a fine run, 'Scotty' Kingsley sent in a hard drive. The ball cannoned off a defender, and Spreadbury headed over the bar from the corner. The game went into an equally ding-dong second half, but as "Gravesend hotly bombarded the visitors' goal", they scored six minutes from time for a 1-0 win – the scorer ex-Addick Tommy Beldham who rejoined the club later this season.

The "Addicker" found the Shrimps a little too much at Gravesend

January 17, 1914

Surprises become routine as Wanderers are routed

A very familiar name still in North West Kent football were Charlton's next opponents at home in the Southern Suburban League – Cray Wanderers, the league leaders. And once again the Addicks upset the form book, with a crushing 4-0 victory.

The crowds seemed to be holding up well for Charlton's first season in senior amateur football, and the game attracted "a fair attendance".

Charlton were now getting independent reports of their games by Kentish Independent reporters rather than only the match reports they filed previously. The KI reporter was effusive about the Addicks' triumph.

"Each week Charlton seem to spring a surprise on their supporters. So confirmed has this habit become that it would be a surprise were a Saturday to pass without a surprise, to use a paradox. The team to beat Cray Wanderers was a harmonious combination. Hampton *(Albert)* could be relied on in goal, Mitchell and Mew kicked strongly and well, and were an admirable pair of backs. The halves did what was required of them without dilly-dallying; they were a useful set. Of the forwards, Kingsley took the eye with fast runs and accurate centres, which were always dangerous. But the whole quintette was a resourceful, penetrating, eager line, who performed their chief business, that of getting goals meritoriously".

The Addicks were two goals up at half-time. Johnny Mitchell put away a penalty after Spreadbury was brought down as he ran on goal, and then his brother Albert added a second.

Despite the Wanderers rallying in the second half, they couldn't stop the Charlton tide. Albert "scored cleverly" to make it 3-0, and then Spreadbury got the fourth in the closing minutes.

Charlton Athletic hooked up a nice little lot of Wandering Crays

January 24, 1914

Kittens hung up as they fail to catch their fish

C atford Southend were destined to play an almost fatal part in the history of the Addicks as just ten years later, an ill-advised move to Catford by the Charlton club – which was really an attempted takeover by Catford Southend – turned out a disaster. The ultimate victims were the Catford club who, once a force in London amateur football, never recovered and went out of existence in February 1927.

Charlton's first senior season now saw them encounter the Kittens' first team. The away match in November at Catford had ended in a 1-1 draw. This time the Kittens had no chance of getting their fish, and the Addicks were decisive winners by 4-0 in a rainsoaked game played on a greasy pitch. The November game had attracted at big crowd at Catford's Ringstead Road ground, and despite the rain, the return at Angerstein Lane also drew the fans, "a very fair crowd" watching the game.

Catford never got into the game and the Addicks pressed for almost the whole of the 90 minutes. The first goal came after the Kittens' goalkeeper was penalised for carrying the ball. From the free kick, 'Mosky' Mills passed the ball to Albert Mitchell who put it into the net.

"The second followed a series of corners, each taken nicely by Kingsley, and Spreadbury had little difficulty beating the custodian", according to the match report.

The third was also the result of an accurate corner from Kingsley with the match report curiously commenting that it "was memorable for the fact that Edwin registered his 'one ewe lamb' of the season". The fourth was from a penalty by Johnny Mitchell after "Spreadbury was clean through, but was pulled down in unceremonious fashion".

The Kittens were caught at Charlton

February 7, 1914

The Addicks cartoons

5,000 crowd turn out for battle with military rivals

I t could be a quirk on the part of the Kentish Independent reporter but the paper reported a 5,000 attendance for the next Southern Suburban game away to the Army Service Corps at Woolwich. The two had long been keen rivals so a big crowd was not unexpected – but hardly of this size. It was certainly an indication of the Addicks' potential to be a top senior amateur club. And the game was given added spice because of the Addicks' 2-1 defeat by ASC just before Christmas.

This time the result was a 1-1 draw in a match that was again very fiercely contested. The midfields dominated the opening stages but then the soldiers went ahead and at half-time the score was 1-0. Despite playing up the slope in the second half, Charlton equalised after ten minutes through a header from R. Harris.

Meanwhile, the running of both a senior and a junior side was causing trouble for Charlton in the Charlton Charity Cup. The B team had beaten Woodside Athletic 2-1 away in the second round, but Woodside protested that the Addicks had played ineligible players i.e. players who had appeared in the senior side.

The Addicks did not dispute the facts but pleaded that without the senior men, they would not have been able to carry out the tie. The B side were thrown out of the cup, and the defeated Woodside took their place for the third round tie against Personnel Ordnance College.

But Charlton came up with a gesture to help defuse the situation by offering to turn out their senior team for a charity match at the end of the season against a selection from the other teams in the competition. And they gave half-a-guinea (52^1/$_2$p) immediately towards the Cup funds.

A level fight between the A.S.C. and Charlton Athletic

February 14, 1914

Comic antics on a pudding of a pitch at Nunhead

Charlton met Nunhead in the Southern Suburban League twice on successive February Saturdays. The first (depicted in the cartoon) was away at Nunhead on February 21 "on a pitch about the consistency of a batter pudding". What the pitch did not do was hinder goalscoring. Charlton were 5-3 up at half-time with a hat-trick from Tommy Beldham and goals from Albert Mitchell and Peter Ladd.

According to the match report, the fifth goal was highly unusual. "Nunhead's backs and goalkeeper all went for the ball. The goalie slipped and the backs floundered all over him. While the whole field was convulsed with laughter at their antics to dig themselves out of the mud, Ladd calmly walked the ball into the net".

Just one goal came in the second half, 'Mosky' Mills scoring from a 'Scotty' Kingsley pass to make it 6-3. With Tufnell Park postponing a London League match, Charlton played Nunhead at Angerstein Lane the next Saturday, and won 2-0 with goals from Ladd and Albert Mitchell.

'Scotty' Kingsley was having a fantastic season for Charlton and apart from his speedy forays on the right wing, he was regularly producing precision crosses for his forwards. For apparently the first time, Charlton Athletic gained national prominence with a piece on Kingsley in the then leading football weekly of its day, Athletic News. It reported:

"A player in London amateur football sought after by the professional clubs is A. Kingsley, of Charlton Athletic. A soldier's son, he was born in the West Indies, but has lived in England since he was a child. It is the possession of Kingsley, and one or two others of his ability, that has enabled Charlton Athletic to make so good a start in senior football".

Another capture by the Charlton Athlete

February 21, 1914

Old Boys put in the boot as Addicks run into trouble

W est London Old Boys 3-0 victory at Angerstein Lane in the London League on a very muddy pitch was not only the first time in the club's nine-year history that the Addicks had gone without a win for three weeks. It also capped a miserable month when unpleasant controversy marred Charlton's highly successful first season in senior football.

The first incident came in a Southern Suburban League match against Metrogas at Angerstein Lane. The teams were level 1-1 when Spreadbury apparently put the ball in the net. Metrogas "protested warmly" that the ball had missed the posts, and the referee, after consulting both linesmen and examining the net, awarded a goal-kick – "an extremely unpopular decision", according to the Independent's reporter.

The game ended 1-1 and the Corner Flag column reported "an ugly demonstration at the close" from the Addicks' fans. But both the Charlton committee and players went to the rescue of the referee and escorted him back to his dressing room at the Angerstein Hotel.

But from that point, the good sense of the committee appeared to have deserted them. They appealed to the Southern Suburban League committee but, then as now, no league was ever going to overturn a result.

Then at Dulwich Hamlet in the Southern Suburban League, "a terrific downpour of rain, accompanied by a gale" chilled the players to the bone. The Addicks were defending a waterlogged goal at the bottom of the slope and appealed for the game to be abandoned. At half-time 2-0 down, they refused to continue and the game was called off. There appears to be no record of any disciplinary action taken against the club.

Charlton 'Addicks badly "outed"

March 21, 1914

Eddie beats seven and bursts net from 30 yards

The Addicks took out their frustrations of a miserable March by thrashing Tufnell Park 7-0 in a London League away game at Finchley. Johnny Mitchell scored four, and Peter Ladd, 'Mosky' Mills and Eddie Marshall the others. According to the Kentish Independent reporter, Eddie's goal was really something to behold.

"He secured the ball on his own goal-line, and, running at top speed, beat no fewer than seven Tufnell players before finishing with a terrific shot from thirty yards range that burst the net, and finally came to rest some forty yards behind the goal. It was a phenomenal effort, and quite deserved the vociferous applause accorded it".

What looked like another big move forward in the Addicks' history came with the disclosure in the Independent's Corner Flag column that "Charlton have secured the Angerstein Lane enclosure as sole tenants for a period of three years ...at a rather big rent, but the committee, who have an eye to business, are going to make it a fine centre".

Evidently the troubled Deptford Invicta club were vacating the stadium, and Corner Flag continued:

"Many improvements are to be made, and during this summer a cricket section will be formed, and matches played there. The support the club has received so far is most satisfactory, and with a good cricket team and a powerful side in football next season they are sure to make things hum in the neighbourhood".

Charlton's future at the Angerstein Lane ground was to be short indeed and far less than the three-year tenancy agreement, with the ground taken over as a petrol dump during the First World War.

The 'Addicks stopped the shouting of Tufnell Park

March 28, 1914

Cray win and Bromley's shirtiness clinches league

Charlton travelled by motor brake to play Cray Wanderers in a game in which they needed one point to win the Eastern Division of the Southern Suburban League. The result was never in doubt, with the Addicks three-nil up in ten minutes. They ran out 5-1 winners, with Spreadbury getting a hat-trick and Peter Ladd getting the other two. The result meant a play-off for the league's overall championship with Old Kingstonians.

Two of the points needed to secure the divisional championship had come rather easily. On the evening of Wednesday, April 15, Charlton had been due to meet Bromley's reserves in the Southern Suburban League, and a crowd of 400 had turned up to watch. According to Corner Flag:

"The club supporters, expecting a good game, showed up in force, and Charlton had their best team out. Bromley, however, although in the dressing room, failed to turn out, and, on inquiry, it was found that they had no jerseys of their own, and refused to play. There was a little confusion when the fact was announced to the crowd by the referee, but Charlton promptly took the matter in hand by paying back the gate money". The league awarded the game and points to the Addicks.

The Cray match coincided with Charlton's promised game with an eleven picked from the Charlton Charity Cup competitors. Obviously Charlton could not keep their promise to provide their senior side but they also seemed to have failed lamentably in even providing their reserve side, with the Addicks turning up at Angerstein Lane "a few men short". The Charity Cup competitors lent players for the Addicks' side, and went on to win the game 2-1.

The " 'Addicks" made a great catch

April 18, 1914

Addicks divide into two in chase for championships

The pressures of playing in two senior leagues and in new cups had mounted up in severe fixture congestion – so much so that Charlton had to play two 'senior teams' on this Saturday. One side was away to Old Kingstonians in the Southern Suburban League decider, and the other faced Wealdstone at home in the London League – a tie with a vital bearing on the Division I championship. Charlton were neck and neck with West London Old Boys at the top of the table, and the Shepherds Bush side had the superior goal average.

According to the Charlton committee: "From the club point of view, the Wealdstone game was the more important, as the club require as many goals as possible to win the London League. But owing to a peculiar ruling of the league at the beginning of the season, the club was compelled to send its stronger team to Kingston, and the 'Sunshine team' were left at home to do their level best to uphold the prestige of the club". What the ruling was, was not explained.

The so-called 'senior' side against Wealdstone was in fact the B side – referred in the match report as the 'Junior Addicks'.

The youngsters did well. They were 1-0 up at half-time and despite being reduced to ten men in the second half held on for the 1-0 victory. But with two more games to go, it was not enough. The Old Boys won the championship on goal average.

At Kingston, in what was obviously an ill-tempered game, the Addicks went down 2-0. The match report commented: "The Athletic had much to complain of in respect to the methods adopted by their opponents, whose idea of fair play did not at all coincide with that of Charlton".

Old Kingey "struck" Charlton Athletic

April 25, 1914

Ten years on, Addicks face the confusion of war

Charlton opened the tenth season of their existence promoted to the London League Premier Division (Amateur Section) but went down in their first game to a 2-0 defeat at Barking on Saturday, August 29. Britain had entered The Great War on Thursday, August 4, after the German invasion of Belgium. The 1914/5 season was to be a strange one indeed. The world of football, just like the rest of Britain, had little foresight of the scale of the tragedy to unfold.

By the time the cartoonist turned his attention to the Addicks for their 7-1 trouncing of Tooting in a home friendly, the confusion of war was wreaking its toll. The Southern Suburban League had already decided to suspend its fixtures while the London League decided to carry on. The Woolwich club, who had taken over Woolwich Arsenal's ground at Plumstead, also suspended their activity. They were to reappear after the war but the long conflict was to sound the death knell of many local clubs whose names have now disappeared in the sands of time – not least Charlton's old rivals, Charlton Amateurs, the successors to the Albion.

The Tooting game had been down as a Southern Suburban fixture but played as a friendly. Tooting took the lead after 15 minutes but Charlton hit back and were 5-1 up at half-time. The seven goals came from Johnny Mitchell (3), 'Mosky' Mills (2), Albert Mitchell and 'Scotty' Kingsley.

During the close season, the club, now in sole possession of the Angerstein ground following the financial problems of their previous partners Deptford Invicta, had invested a lot of money and time in it. A stream of volunteers worked to improve the stands and banking to bring the capacity up to 4,000 – their efforts were to be short-lived indeed.

What the 'Addicks caught

September 19, 1914

Barking revenge as London League struggles on

This season marked Charlton's first entries into the FA Cup and the FA Amateur Cup. Charlton should have drawn Ashford Railway Works in the first qualifying round of the FA Cup but the railwaymen scratched the fixture. Charlton went on to make their debut in the competition against Dartford. They were drawn as the home club but "owing to financial difficulties" switched the tie to Dartford. The game ended in a 0-0 draw and the replay was lost 2-1, again at Dartford.

Meanwhile, the war was wreaking havoc on the Amateur Cup with the first draw postponed because of 50 clubs withdrawing or breaking up.

Charlton this season were entered in two divisions of the London League, the first team in the Premier Division (Amateur Section) and a second team, now called the 'A' team, in the First Division. The Premier Division was structured into twin sections, one called the Professional Section taking in reserve sides of some of the capital's Football League clubs, and the other the Amateur Section with a separate fixture list.

The first team, having lost at Barking in the opening game, now exacted revenge in the return match, winning by 6-1 with two goals each from 'Mosky' Mills, Johnny Mitchell and S. Chaplin. But the steady drain of war was taking its toll on the London League in spite of the decision to continue fixtures. Woolwich and Kingston-on-Thames had dropped out of the Premier Amateur Section, as had Wealdstone, Cricklewood Generals and Woolwich Polytechnic from the First Division. Army Service Corps had withdrawn from the First Division on the outbreak of war. Woolwich was one of the country's main military areas and the many army teams in the area had pulled out of all local competitions.

The 'Addicks captured the Barkers

October 31, 1914

Kittens beat the 10 men as row divides newspaper

The first effects of war on the playing strength of Charlton were now being reported in the pages of the Kentish Independent. In an A team London League First Division match against Catford Southend, the Charlton side turned up at the Kittens' Ringstead Road ground with only ten men. The week before both the A side and their London League opponents Tufnell Park had also turned up missing players, although by how many was not reported.

Although a man short, the A team were two nil up against the Kittens in 35 minutes through Cross and Herbert Franklin, before going down to a 3-2 defeat. Meanwhile, the first team were playing a peculiar fixture at the Angerstein ground – a friendly against Burberry's Athletic from Acton which they won 2-1. It was strange because Burberry's were due to be their first-ever opponents in the FA Amateur Cup the following Saturday in the third qualifying round but had scratched because their officials had said they were unable to raise a team.

The Corner Flag column in the Independent was showing signs of serious tension between the columnist Stanley Hudson and the paper's editor. Hudson clung to the view that football at all levels should carry on as a recreation in time of war. The editor had already inserted a statement in the column that he disagreed with this. Now the Under Secretary of State for War put out a national statement which said that, while the military authorities did not object to occasional recreation, he thought professional football should be discontinued and professional footballers should enlist in the forces. The KI editor put a second statement into the Corner Flag column stressing his strong agreement with the government.

The Kittens "pinched" the 'Addicks

November 14, 1914

Addicks play as if they had been working all night

By the time the next cartoon appeared in the new year of 1915, Charlton were still struggling on. The home London League Premier Division game against Finchley ended in a 5-0 defeat. Again the Addicks started a game a man short. Charlton's published team line-ups were now fairly irregular in the pages of the Independent, but the team was given for this game and it showed many regulars missing – whether through pressure of war work or joining the forces.

According to the Corner Flag report of the game: "It is very evident that the Charlton Athletic players are feeling the extra pressure of work being caused by the war, for they played last Saturday, as though they had been working all night". Cash shortages were now hitting the club, caused by the outlay on the Angerstein ground set against the reduced attendances of wartime. The particularly bad weather of the wartime winter did not help either with several home games cancelled. The club's first actual game in the FA Amateur Cup saw them drawn against City of Westminster at home in the fourth qualifying round. They won 6-1 but then made their exit from the competition, losing 4-1 at home to Grays Athletic in the first round, on the Saturday previous to the Finchley game.

The FA had a few weeks before called a special meeting to decide to carry on with the FA and FA Amateur cups, and had also put forward the idea of a footballers' battalion for Kitchener's army.

The Woolwich sports supply firm, H. Gradidge & Sons, better known for its famous cricketing gear, placed an advert in the Independent to send footballs to the Expeditionary Force or to any part of the Empire, packed free and carriage paid, 8 shillings (40p) to 13s 6d (67½p).

Finchley made a fine catch at Charlton

January 9, 1915

Charlton close down as Catford games end in farce

This was the last cartoon our unknown cartoonist drew of a Charlton game – a 6-2 home victory in the London League Premier Division over Catford Southend. Other football cartoons appeared until May, and he also drew cartoons poking fun at the Germans and Kaiser Bill – in very naive taste, looking at them from modern eyes. His last cartoon – a non-football one – appeared on Friday, October 22, 1915, and then he disappears forever from the pages of the Independent.

Neither team was at full strength with Catford having to enlist their goalkeeper and trainer in their forward line. Charlton were 2-0 up at half-time through goals by Moore, only for Catford to pull back the two goals soon after the restart. Then Charlton ran away with the game with four more goals – by Moore, twice, 'Scotty' Kingsley and 'Mosky' Mills. But our cartoonist's comment was totally wide of the mark. Almost everything was wrong with the Addicks and wartime had wreaked its toll.

The following Saturday, Catford and Charlton met at Ringstead Road, Catford, and the game turned into a debacle. An obviously even more weakened Charlton team found themselves 7-0 down at the interval in terrible weather conditions and refused to play the second half. Just one more match was played, a friendly away at Tooting, which Charlton won 5-1, before the committee decided in March to suspend the club.

The last game played was a charity match on Saturday, April 17, between Charlton and a representative team from the Charlton Charity Cup clubs. The Addicks won 4-1 with a hat-trick by Johnny Mitchell and a goal from Harrison. It was their last ever game at Angerstein Lane with the newly-renovated ground now to meet its fate as a petrol dump.

What's wrong with the 'Addicks? Nothing!

February 6, 1915

WAR ....AND

The situation which had led to the closedown of Charlton Athletic was summed up by Corner Flag in these words: "I feel sure that all classes of football players in Woolwich and the surrounding districts will learn with deep regret that Charlton Athletic have had to throw up the sponge and discontinue operations for this season. There has been no break in the ranks, the players and committee have stuck together well, and until the last few weeks have honourably met their engagements and responsibilities. But a large percentage of the players work in Government 'shops', and keen pressure applied to every man to work as long as he could and permission to be absent has often been refused. The consequence has been that the club committee could never rely upon the team they picked, substitutes have had to be found at an hour's notice, and points that in the ordinary way would easily have been picked up have been thrown away. I am very sorry for the club, for at one time they had every appearance of winning the London League".

But Corner Flag was as unaware of the duration of modern warfare as the rest of his generation. He added: "I trust next season will see them in fettle once more".

Meanwhile the gaps in the depleted sports pages of the Independent began to be filled in eery contrast with the pictures of the young men of the district who had died on land and at sea. Every week, on and on, showing what a terrible toll the Great War took.

We know from a wartime report that most of the Charlton players, such as Johnny Mitchell, enlisted in the army but not all their names nor their numbers. A report from the club after the war, whose figures included

REBIRTH

both players and members, stated: "We have a war record of which we are justly proud. Some thirty of our members served in HM Forces on the various battlefields of Europe. We regret that of this number, three have made the supreme sacrifice, while six others have been wounded".

The club reformed at a meeting held on Wednesday, January 9, 1918, at the Mission Hall, Troughton Road, Charlton, with "a large number of enthusiasts attending". Eddie Heath once again became secretary and a programme of friendlies to raise funds for wartime charities was planned from February. The first was appropriately against an army team, the Army Ordnance Department, at the Rectory Field, Blackheath, in aid of the Royal Dockyard Benevolent Fund for entertaining and providing comforts for sick and wounded sailors and soldiers. Some 150 men came from the local hospitals to attend the match. Charlton, captained by Eddie Marshall, won 7-1 but the result was almost immaterial.

From then on, in the reports in the Independent, the reader can see the power surging back into the club, and the symbolism of football as the country emerged from the horror of the Great War. In all, Charlton raised some £800 for the charities – a very large sum in those days.

And in the Woolwich area, there was a gap to fill – the Football League gap left by the departure of Woolwich Arsenal in 1913. After two seasons of friendlies, the club, complete with a new ground, The Valley, gained admission to the Kent League for the 1919/20 season. The next season, 1920/21, saw the club rise to the Southern League. Then for the 1921/22 season, the club was elected to the Third Division of the Football League. Out of the rebirth of the club had come a footballing miracle.

1905/6

The first known photograph of Charlton Athletic. The players' names are not given

1906/7
Back row: J. Merryweather, H. Hughes, W. Wilson, W. Higgs, W. King (Captain), J. Sudds, H. T. Wells (President)
Middle: E. Holt (First Aid), J. Mitchell, A. Buckenham, W. Bonner, W. Pirie, E. Marshall, J. Mitchell (senior), J. Mackenzie (Hon. Sec.)
Front: C. Broom, A. Mills, A. Thomas

FOUNDING YEARS BEFORE THE GREAT WAR

1908/9

Back row: J. Merryweather, J. Garrett (President), W. Bonner, H. Hughes, W. King (Captain), E. Sudds, W. Wilson, W. Pirie senior, J. Mackenzie (Hon. Sec.)
Middle: J. Sudds, C. Broom, A. Mills, J. Keys, A. Egan
Front: J. Sharp, E. Marshall, A. Ellis

1913/14

Fourth/back row: E. Hunt, E. Cross, A. Hunt, A. Hampton, S. Owen, H. Gritton, A. Watt, E. Chapman
Third row: W. Budden, E. Chick, J. Gritton, J. Earlie, H. Saywood, S. Mew, G. Farrer, J. Merryweather, J. Scrivner
Second row: J. Wotten, W. Blagrove, A. Kingsley, E. Marshall, A. Mills, H. Franklin, J. Mitchell, H. Hughes, E. Heath (Hon. Sec.)
Front: E. Hornsby, A. Mitchell

The legend
of the
Addicker

*Arthur Bryan
– the fishmonger
who started
the legend*

The fishmonger cartoon figure was not the imagination of the cartoonist. It was based on a real life person – Arthur 'Ikey' Bryan who owned a fish shop in East Street (now Eastmoor Street), at the heart of the riverside community where the Charlton Athletic club was born. In modern parlance, Ikey was one of the first sponsors of the club. His sponsorship took the unusual form of fish and chip suppers for the boys and their opponents. But he also helped in more straightforward ways as well, shelling out to help meet the running costs of the club.

Ikey's life was a colourful one but ultimately poignant and sad.

He was born in 1882 and took over the fish shop at 77 East Street in 1907. By that time, he was already a keen supporter of the new team formed by a dozen or so youngsters in the area who gathered one summer night – June 9, 1905 – under a street lamp and enthusiastically discussed forming a club.

The fish and chips the boys consumed led to a lasting legacy for the club – its nickname. A year after he took over the shop, the Haddock nickname first appeared in the local press. Soon the spelling changed into a version based on the South London accent of those days – the Addicks.

The Addick nickname came fully into public prominence in 1909 at the final of the Woolwich Cup, played at Creed's Farm, Cemetery Lane (see page 22). By that time Arthur was vice president of the club and several large haddocks from his shop were paraded on poles by Arthur and fellow fans around the ground. Arthur was part of a small closeknit community that gave immense moral and practical help to the young boys who formed the new Charlton Athletic.

Living next door were the greengrocers, the Bradshaws, and next to the Bradshaws, the butchery business run by the King family. His shop was bounded on the other side by the house of the Buddens, a family who sold ribbons and buttons. Together with Arthur's shop, they are now the site of a Ford car spares business. All these families were an integral part of the early history of the Charlton Athletic team.

The Bradshaws also owned the hauliers along the road, and it was they who moved the goal posts for the games on Siemens Field from weekday storage in the Buddens' back garden. They later provided horse brake transport from the Crown pub for away games.

Sam Budden kept the team's boots in his garden shed. Goalkeeper Bill 'Bodger' King – an early club captain – came from the butchery family.

The club's first president was Harry Wells, landlord of the Crown pub in East Street. Tom Sullivan, landlord of the Prince of Wales in West Street (now Westmoor Street), Fred Williams, the local newsagent and

Addicks whose forbears helped create Charlton Athletic. Back, from left: Frank Mercer, Kathy Mercer, Brian Kinsey, Barry Martin, Annette Mercer. Middle: Sarah Mercer, Kate Mercer, Max Martin. Front: Andrew Mercer

The site of Arthur Bryan's fish shop at 77 East Street - now premises for a car spares firm in the renamed Eastmoor Street. His shop would have been situated just to the left of the entrance

confectioner, and John Garrett, the owner of the Sunderland shipbreaking yard on the Thames off North Street at the end of West Street were also part of this band of supporters. John was to become the club's second president, and, on his death in 1912, he was succeeded by John Mitchell, father of the Mitchell brothers.

The financial support these businesses gave was constant and extended beyond the tragic years of the First World War when most other local clubs disappeared for ever. They were behind the postwar discovery of the club's new home, the chalkpit that was to become the biggest ground in the country, The Valley. The redoubtable Sam Budden masterminded much of the excavation and Bradshaw carts were used to cart the rubble away. Fred Williams and Tom Sullivan were among the seven backers of the 1921 share fundraising to support the entry into the Football League.

Ikey's tenure of his shop was to last until the 1930s, but his immense love of the club was to end in personal tragedy and sadness.

He married twice. His second wife was Dorothy Langdon but, in the 1920s, Arthur ran into financial trouble – ironically through trying to act as a guarantor at the bank of Charlton Athletic's debts as a fledgling Football League club. A description of these difficulties appears in the book Battle for the Valley, by Rick Everitt (1991). Arthur, who had been given the catering concession for the new Valley, had to ask the board in August 1922 to be released from the guarantee. He had hoped to become a director, but that ambition was forever lost. He was eventually reduced to living for some time in the 1930s in a garden allotment. He died in

1956 at King's College Hospital, Dulwich, and is now interred in a family vault in Charlton Cemetery opposite Charlton Park.

Closely intertwined with the life of the Bryan family were the Buddens. Arthur and Dorothy had one child Kathleen (Kathy) who was born in 1924, and, at the age of six, was taken in by Sam and Gertrude Budden.

The Buddens had four children. Gladys (who wrapped the fish in Arthur's shop), Bill, Fred and Dolly. Bill married Rose Etherton whose sister Daisy married Bob Kinsey. They had a son – Brian, later to become one of the most famous of Charlton footballers. Daisy and Bob went to live in Bill's house and so Brian Kinsey came to live with the Budden family. The families were also related through Rose and Daisy to the Marshall family of Charlton's early history, who were local coal merchants.

The Budden family moved together after the First World War to 25 Charlton Lane opposite the Royal Oak. The Second World War was to bring tragedy to them. On the same raid that damaged the Royal Oak in 1944, number 25 was completely demolished. Five of the family died that night, including Bill, Fred's wife Flo and Dolly's husband Syd.

It was Kathy who managed to pull Gladys out of the rubble of the blast. Survivors included Fred's son Keith Budden, and Dolly's son Barry Martin. Brian Kinsey, then just a boy, escaped alive but still carries pieces of shrapnel in his leg. Bill can be seen in the team picture on page 123.

The Crown pub was also a casualty of the Second World War, being hit successively by a bomb and a flying landmine.

Kathleen married Frank Mercer in April, 1947, and they were to run for many years a famous dancing school at Bickley in Bromley, Kent.

Kathy and Gladys (Gladys Jeavons) are alive today at the time of writing and Kathy is a season ticket holder at The Valley as is her husband Frank, her son Andrew Mercer, his wife Annette, and their two daughters, Kate and Sarah. Andrew continues the proud tradition of his grandfather Arthur by being a leading sponsor of the modern Charlton Athletic.

As with Arthur's descendants, the Budden descendants also continue the proud tradition of the founding families and are supporters to this day. Barry Martin and his grandson Max (see picture, page 125), and Keith Budden and his son Nigel are all part of the closeknit Addicker group, and Brian Kinsey joins with the group before and after every home game.

Arthur Bryan – the Addicker – may be a longlost figure of the club's distant past but this tangible connection lives on. A living link to the founding days of the club in that longlost Thamesside community of which he was so prominent and famous a part.

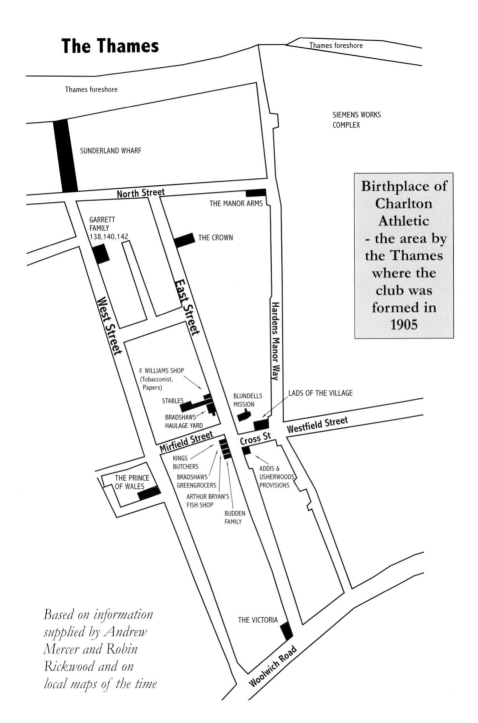

The Thames

Thames foreshore

Thames foreshore

SIEMENS WORKS
COMPLEX

SUNDERLAND WHARF

North Street

THE MANOR ARMS

GARRETT
FAMILY
138,140,142

THE CROWN

West Street

East Street

Hardens Manor Way

F. WILLIAMS SHOP
(Tobacconist,
Papers)

STABLES

BRADSHAWS
HAULAGE YARD

BLUNDELLS
MISSION

LADS OF THE VILLAGE

Westfield Street

Mirfield Street

Cross St

KINGS
BUTCHERS

BRADSHAWS
GREENGROCERS

ADDIS &
USHERWOODS
PROVISIONS

THE PRINCE
OF WALES

ARTHUR BRYAN'S
FISH SHOP

BUDDEN
FAMILY

Birthplace of Charlton Athletic - the area by the Thames where the club was formed in 1905

THE VICTORIA

Woolwich Road

Based on information supplied by Andrew Mercer and Robin Rickwood and on local maps of the time